Kitchen Witchcraft: Spells & Charms

Kitchen Witchcraft: Spells & Charms

Rachel Patterson

Winchester, UK
Washington, USA

First published by Moon Books, 2018
Moon Books is an imprint of John Hunt Publishing Ltd., No. 3 East Street, Alresford
Hampshire SO24 9EE, UK
office1@jhpbooks.net
www.johnhuntpublishing.com
www.moon-books.net

For distributor details and how to order please visit the 'Ordering' section on our website.

Text copyright: Rachel Patterson 2017

ISBN: 978 1 78535 768 8
978 1 78535 769 5 (ebook)
Library of Congress Control Number: 2017950189

A CIP catalogue record for this book is available from the British Library.

Design: Stuart Davies

Printed and bound by CPI Group (UK) Ltd, Croydon, CR0 4YY, UK

We operate a distinctive and ethical publishing philosophy in
all areas of our business, from our global network of authors to
production and worldwide distribution.

Contents

Who am I?

I am a witch ... have been for a very long time, not the green skinned warty kind obviously but the real sort. I am also a working wife and mother who has been lucky enough to write and have published a book or three. I love to learn, I love to study and have done so from books, online resources, schools and wonderful mentors over the years and continue to learn every day but have learnt the most from getting outside and doing it. I like to laugh, bake and eat cake ...

I am High Priestess of the Kitchen Witch Coven and an Elder at the online Wyrd Witches/Kitchen Witch School.

I also have a regular Hedge Witch blog on Witches & Pagans and Beneath the Moon blog on Patheos Pagan.

My website: www.rachelpatterson.co.uk
Facebook: www.facebook.com/rachelpattersonbooks
My personal blog: www.tansyfiredragon.blogspot.co.uk
Email: kitchenwitchhearth@yahoo.com
www.kitchenwitchhearth.net
www.kitchenwitchuk.blogspot.co.uk
www.facebook.com/kitchenwitchuk

My craft is a combination of old religion Witchcraft, Kitchen Witchery, Hedge Witchery and folk magic. My heart is that of a Kitchen Witch.

Acknowledgements

Special thanks must go to:

Pete for his continued support, encouragement and ability to understand how my brain works.

Emma for her beautiful and talented artistic skills (the cauldron sketch inside this book is her work).

Ben for reading through the manuscript to check my grammar and spelling, and for the additional sketches of dinosaurs and exploding chickens to make me smile.

Vaughn for doing an excellent copy edit and adding entertaining comments that made me laugh.

Warning

If you are handling herbs, plants, flowers and essential oils please be aware of any allergies.

Check that you have identified the plants correctly.

With essential oil especially (and some plants) check allergies and toxicity.

Some undiluted oils can cause nasty reactions when they come in contact with skin.

Pregnant ladies, elderly and young children should be extremely careful when handling essential oils – check with a qualified practitioner before using.

Kitchen Witchcraft: Spells & Charms

A spell can be worked in many ways from a simple pointing of the finger to a complicated ritual involving lots of tools, herbs and crystals and of course any variation in between. As a Kitchen Witch, I do prefer to keep things simple so I am sharing my Kitchen folk magic spells with you but also delving into different types of spells, how you put them together, how to work with them and what you need.

There are a lot of things in the universe that we don't understand. When something is meant to happen, it will, whether you cast a spell or not. But you can help it on its way by guiding and encouraging it and maybe even tweaking events a little too. What will happen for sure is the boost of confidence and happy buzz you will receive as you cast the spell. You also get the positive vibe that you are putting something into action.

What exactly is a spell?

From the dictionary (which is always interesting to see) the definition of the word 'spell':

> *A spell is a series of words that has magical powers. If you're under a spell, then what you do is out of your control — your thoughts and actions are dictated by the spell.*
>
> *Spell can refer to the magic words you say, or it can describe being under the influence of those words.*

Quite possibly the most common question I get asked when people discover I am a witch is, "do you cast spells?" That's after the questions, "are you evil" and "can you turn me into a toad?" And to be honest although it is a part of my way of life to do so it is not something I do every single day. If I have an issue or a problem then I tend to look for the mundane solution first.

However, it is a wonderful way to bring about things that you desire or need and to create a better life, not just for you but for your family and friends. Maybe even help the planet a little bit too. If you have the magic at your fingertips why not use it? But remember, that with great power comes great responsibility.

In its most simple form a spell is the wish or desire to bring about change whether it is in your life or that of others. Add to that wish your own will, intent, belief and energy and you can make change happen. Although it sounds straightforward a successful spell-working takes thought, focus and energy. If you don't believe in what you are doing then the chances are that the result will be non-existent. Badly constructed spells or those cast in anger have a habit of going wrong, sometimes with disastrous results. Spells in general do have a habit of 'doing their own thing' and often have unexpected results. Fundamentally, I wholeheartedly believe that the universe knows best and what you want isn't always what you need. There is a very big difference between 'want' and 'need'. The universe has a habit of stepping into magic and diverting it …

Anyone can cast a spell but the result will differ depending on the strength of will, intent, focus, energy and commitment to backing up the spell with actions. For example, there is no point casting a spell to find a job and then not actually applying for any. The universe isn't going to drop your dream job straight into your lap.

You must believe the spell will work, any negative thoughts about the outcome of your spell, before or after you have cast it, will have an impact on the results. If you think your spell won't work, it won't, the energy you put into the spell will follow your thoughts and affect the outcome. If your thoughts are negative, the outcome will not be as you intended. So, after you cast a spell only allow your thoughts and actions to be positive ones which will reinforce your spell.

And just to be really confusing there is also the train of thought that once you cast a spell you should forget about it completely. Follow your intuition on this one; I think it also varies depending on the spell because some workings need keeping an eye on and others may also need a regular boost of energy.

Visualisation is also key; you need to be able to clearly picture your desired result when you are working magic. Using finding a job as an example again; you receive a chance to interview for a position; you decide to cast a simple spell to secure a successful outcome from that interview. During the spell you may wish to visualise yourself at the interview, answering all the questions with ease and confidence and with a smile on your face. See yourself wearing the clothes you plan to wear and shaking hands with the interviewer. Then maybe you visualise accepting the position and seeing your name on office stationery or something of a similar nature. By visualising yourself in the position you have put your consciousness there, now all your physical body must do is follow that path.

Where do you work your magic?

In the days before we had teenage children the conservatory on our house was given over to me to use as my witchy room, referred to by my husband as 'The Bat Cave'. Inside I had a large wooden table to work on and a huge dresser to use as an apothecary cupboard for all my herbs and magical supplies. There was also space for a large working altar to put my spells and charms once they were set up to 'do their thing'. The doors open out to the garden and it was indeed a very magical place to work. I could create spells and charms on the table using items selected from my cupboards or direct from the garden. Often working out in the garden too, using a big flat stone collected from Tintagel, Cornwall as my altar.

Altars also appeared all over the house and the garden, each one for a specific purpose. Certain spells would be laid to 'prove' at the feet of Ganesha on his altar. Others would be placed in front of the Cailleach on her altar; whilst some were laid out in the garden or on the kitchen altar.

Now we have a teenager who is about to embark on a college course for fashion. This has meant me handing over my bat cave to be converted into a sewing room ... alas alack ...

Now my magical workings must be conducted in the dining room and my apothecary has been significantly scaled down. My altar size has also diminished and I am having to use the altar dedicated to the Cailleach as a working altar too. But do you know what? I am OK with it. There are priorities in life and this is how it needs to be for now. And let's face it, I am a Kitchen Witch, I am adaptable and flexible and can work with the challenges!

I also work from home and have a small 'office' in the bay window upstairs in our house. I found myself working magic there last week. Sitting at my desk I needed a spell so I worked some sigil magic, right there sat in front of my laptop and keyboard I cleared some space. Grabbing a pen and some paper from the printer I drew sigils. On the spot, no preparation, no ritual bathing, no cleansing and purifying, no preparation. And it worked perfectly (phew!).

Magic for me is often also worked in my kitchen. Every meal I make has added sprinkles of positive energy. Each cake I bake is made with love included. When I vacuum and dust the house I work magic as I go.

Whilst I have been known to set up elaborate altars and spells with several ingredients and a bit of preparation, it is not something I do often. I am more of a practical hands on, working mum who has to use what she has to hand and in the few precious moments of free time.

I like simple. I like practical. I like hassle-free spell work. If I see a spell that lists 57 different ingredients and takes four hours to set up I am very unlikely to even read past the first page let alone attempt it. (That's not to say it won't be a good spell or work for others, it just isn't for me.)

For me, keeping spell work simple and uncomplicated means there is less chance for it to go haywire.

Spells have an uncanny habit of working in very unexpected ways so I feel that the less there is within it, the less there is to go wrong.

Does the setting have to be grand though? Do you have to work magic on a gold encrusted, velvet draped altar? Will the spell work better if you are standing in a grove of ancient oaks? Is it important to create a mystical atmosphere and sacred space before working magic? I would say: No, no, no and no ... Although to be fair my house is regularly smudged and cleansed and full of enough incense on a regular basis to choke a whole coven of witches. So the space that I work magic in is very well versed with magical energy.

In my very humble opinion and based on many years of working spells, I firmly believe that the setting is not as important as the will and the intent. Not everyone has the luxury of space to set up grand magical workings and not everyone can do so or would want to in front of others in a shared house.

My thoughts are ... the magic is within YOU, trust your intuition and work with spells in the space that suits you best.

Disclaimer: Just remember that magic is a gift, sometimes a very strong one and spells carry power – be responsible ...

Sign it with your own name

Add in your own unique and individual flair to make the magic truly yours.

Do you follow recipes, spells and ritual instructions written by others to the letter? Do you make your own tweaks or do you just 'do your own thing' completely? Now, I realise how ironic this sounds laid out in a book filled with spells but these are here for you as a guide, a place to start from. My style of spell writing may not resonate with everyone, so add your own spin to them.

I think the same applies to magical workings and rituals of any kind. If we add our own spin to the structure borrowed from others or write our own from scratch, it will have our own unique flair to it.

When I first began my witchcraft journey the only real structured learning available to me was in the form of Wicca, which generally has specific outlines and guides which I followed diligently. I look back now at the rituals and spells I worked then and I can't see myself in them. But my pathway veered off into the Wild/Kitchen/Hedge witch area a long time ago.

We all need to start somewhere and having that original guidance was what I required at the time. Without specific instructions, who knows what magical mayhem I could have caused? With a few 'banish all negativity' spells that were performed I did indeed create a bit of chaos. Even with the best worded and carefully planned spell, the universe often has its own ideas about how the result should play out ...

There is, of course, no short cut to experience and I am very glad that I followed all the guidelines in the beginning. However, as time went on my learning progressed and my experience with it, I gradually learnt to follow my intuition. Now when I write a ritual or a spell it is unique to me and with my own peculiarities.

If I do use structured writings from others to work a spell or ritual then I always add in my own spin. Mostly because I am not comfortable with a lot of ceremony (and by that, I mean I am fairly lazy). I don't want to take hours preparing, spend a fortune on ceremonial gowns or purchase twenty-seven rare and exotic ingredients from across the globe. That's not to say you shouldn't – if it works for you go for it. But by adding my own twists or writing from the heart I make the magic my own, it has my individual energy to it.

I always encourage students (at our online Kitchen Witch School) to write their own spells or rituals because if you are doing so then it will be totally yours, it doesn't matter how simple or how fancy it is. The fact that you have written and designed it from scratch will mean that is has, I think anyway, more magical oomph because YOU put the effort in and it has your style all over it.

If you are starting your journey then it is good to begin with the works and ideas of others. But I would still encourage you to trust your intuition and make tweaks if you feel the need. And if you don't have all the ingredients for a spell then use what you do have. Maybe if the way a circle casting or quarter call is carried out doesn't suit you, then change it. Don't do anything that feels wrong, switch it up so that it feels right for you.

Sign the magic with your own name.

Working with the Craft

Working with the Craft is very personal; everyone will walk their own pathway and take a very individual journey.

I don't believe there is a right way or a wrong way to work with anything within the Craft, whether it is how to cleanse and charge your crystals, how to make a poppet or what herb to use in spell work.

There are lists on the internet and there are books a plenty – (including this one) all of which have guidance and suggestions but, and here's the thing, no one person should tell you that you MUST do something a certain way. We can only share our personal experiences and the knowledge that we have learnt, but only as an opinion or an option, NOT a definitive.

I firmly believe that each person should trust their own intuition and be guided by pure instinct when working magic. Just because a book or the internet or someone else says "do it this way" does not mean it will be the right way for everyone.

Of course, there are 'standard' ways of working things, such as the order a ritual goes in but even then, who says it must be that way?

Obviously, there are some things that are sensible and it would be irresponsible not to follow some of the guidelines. For example, if you are working strong magic then it is advisable to cast a circle for your own protection and the protection of others. If you are new to the Craft then be very careful when working your first magic spell, go for something simple and nothing too complicated.

Even when working with something that is set like moon phases you can still wangle it to work for you – it's just a matter of tweaking the wording.

However, with the areas of magic such as herbs (magical not medicinal) and crystals – these items have a spirit and will tell us what needs to be done with them ... herbs and crystals do not read books, they don't know what the '*standard*' is!

Do what works for you.

Do spells work?

In my experience, provided they have been thought through, worked out and performed properly – yes!

You do have to consider that the universe can be a total git and often has a habit of interfering. Spells also tend to work in unexpected ways, so just be prepared.

Why didn't my spell work?

If you set a spell in motion and it doesn't seem to have worked there may be a number of reasons. Occasionally it just doesn't – even the most skilled spell caster won't have a 100% success rate.

Maybe your spell worked but not in the way you wanted? The universe does like to interfere or maybe you weren't specific enough. Make sure you are clear and concise.

Are you familiar with the techniques used? Maybe you didn't fully understand the working or you might just need more experience. Start from the beginning.

Were you really committed to the outcome? Or were you perhaps a bit half-hearted about it?

Did you set any time frame? If you didn't specify that you needed the spell to work quickly then it may take it's time.

Did you ask deity or the universe for something? If you did, remember that a request can also receive the answer 'no' ...

Did you request assistance from deity, the divine or angels? Particularly if you don't have a relationship with them or didn't give an offering in exchange for your thanks they might not be interested in helping.

Was your desired outcome realistic? Working a spell to become a real live princess ain't gonna happen ...

Did you raise a good strong amount of energy? Was it a

tornado of power or a gnat's sneeze?

Do you doubt your skills? Did you send out conflicting messages?

Be confident in what you do.

Take responsibility

A little side note on the term 'an harm to none'. This is often used at the end of spells as a disclaimer. For instance, if you cast a money spell but you don't want to gain the money by someone dying and leaving it to you in their will you could use 'an harm to none' as an escape clause. However, bear in mind that although this does reduce accidents it can also neutralise the spell in some cases. You are telling the magic to work but also restricting it. I don't mean by stopping it from killing people (coz that is wrong, definitely wrong) but by curtailing the energy from causing anyone inconvenience. Properly put together and well thought out spells should not back fire in any way, so you shouldn't need to cover yourself. If you work a spell to gain more money and you get given overtime instead of your colleague then the spell has worked, but someone else lost out in the process. You must take responsibility for that, it is a cruel world sometimes and you need to decide whether you can live with it.

Ethics

This will depend on your own personal feelings. The suggested guideline is: Do not cast spells to alter the will of another or to cause harm. Also, to never cast spells for others without their permission even if your intent is pure. But … and here is the thing, you are the one deciding to cast the spell so it is your choice to make. You may feel that the need is justified to cast a bad luck spell on another or even a curse; it's not my place to judge or to tell you what you can and can't do. Just make sure you think it through properly and be mindful of any return. It also pays to bear in mind if you do cast a curse or a hex be aware that if the person you are sending it to realises where it came from they may very well send it back ...

Intent

For me this is key to any good spell, you need to have solid intent for the magic to happen. And by intent, I mean the determination, intention and purpose to make this work. You also need to have the will; that pure resolve, drive and motivation to back it up.

Where to start?

So, you've decided to go ahead and cast a spell, where do you start? Here are some basic guidelines to help you write your first spell.

Purpose

What you need to decide first is what the purpose of you spell is but also have you covered all the other options first?

Is there a mundane solution that will bring the same outcome?

Intent

If you are set to work a spell, make sure you put some thought into it and ask yourself if you are willing to put the work into it to back it up and follow it through.

It is a pointless waste of time and makes a mockery of the Craft if you just go into it half-heartedly.

Then ...

Write down your intent and be as detailed as you can. If your intent is to find a job, be very specific about what job it is that you want/need and when you would like to have the job by. When writing out your intent think about answers to these questions:

- *Who? What? Where? When? Why? How?*
- Some answers you may write down are:

- Who? – Me
- What? – A new position of employment
- Where? – Within "such and such" a company
- When? – October 2017 – always put a specific date of when you need the spell to manifest
- Why? – To gain secure employment and financial stability
- How? – By being a successful candidate at the job interview

When I cast my first spell it took me forever ... I researched, I wrote it all out in detail and spent ages setting it all up. And yes, I felt pretty silly doing it. It was a slow process but each spell I cast after that became more refined and generally faster to work. These days I tend to work more "off the cuff' and don't write it all down first, and I follow my intuition and let it guide me as to where the spell wants to take me and what it needs. This sounds in complete contradiction to my strong guidelines above but it comes with experience and I always make sure I am still very precise with my wordings and my intent. In fact, I encourage you to follow your intuition when putting a spell together, be guided by what words, herbs and oils you need.

Trust your inner voice. Just make sure you are specific ...

You don't have to write a beautiful sonnet or rhyming poem to go with your spell but the words must have meaning. Your aim here is to speak your intent and tell the universe what it is you desire. This can be a chant that rhymes or just words from the heart, whichever you chose the universe will hear and respond.

Choose the type of magic you want to work with whether it is candle magic, a cord spell, creating a witch bottle – whatever method feels right for that spell. (More details on types of spell further on in this book.)

Next you need to gather together the 'ingredients' and that might be a candle, corresponding herbs and/or oils, paper, pens, matches. Write a list of everything you will need and gather them all together in one place. You might even want to decorate your altar or space to tie in with your spell work (this isn't essential but always an option).

Choose your ingredients carefully, trust your intuition and be guided about what items you need and what they will bring to the spell-working.

You can layer the power of your spell magic by using corresponding items such as working the spell on a certain day of the week or phase of the moon. Spices, herbs and oils can all be added in for extra power. Using a particular colour candle or altar cloth will also boost the magic.

Your ingredients will also need charging or activating before you use them. They need to know what magic you require them to work. I like to hold the item (herb, crystal, candle, whatever it might be) in my hand and draw energy up from the earth and down from the sky channelling it through me adding my intent and visualising my desire. I send the energy down through my hands and into the item. NEVER draw energy from your own body because you will end up exhausted. Mother Nature is more than happy to give you her energy, just use your body to channel it.

Note

I don't believe herbs for magical use need to be expensive or picked at dawn by a virgin maiden wearing red silk underwear … Use what you have to hand. Grow your own herbs and dry them or forage in the woods and by the roadsides. Purchase bunches of fresh herbs at farmers' markets or big bags of dried herbs at Asian markets or in your local supermarket. If you are worried about how 'pure' they are then just cleanse them by visualising a clear white light removing any negative energy. You are going to charge the ingredients for your spell with your intent anyway.

I also tend to avoid any spell that lists 73 different ingredients including exotic ones that I would have to order online and have shipped halfway across the world. Personally, I prefer to work with what I can easily and cheaply source; call me lazy, call me tight or call me a Kitchen Witch – I don't care, it works for me!

The same goes for candles and materials; in an ideal world, I would love to be able to afford beautifully crafted eco-friendly candles. But they aren't always readily available and they are not usually very affordable (I do understand why: The time and cost of ingredients used). I work with candles purchased from 99p/dollar shops and often find candle holders and scarves to use for altar cloths in thrift/charity stores. I have never had any problems and to date have not been struck down by the gods for using such items. Use what you have to hand, use what you can afford.

It sounds like a lot of work and sometimes it can be depending on how complicated you want to make the spell. However, it doesn't have to be and I encourage anyone who is inexperienced or unsure to start simply. All you need to cast a spell is to say a wish to the moon, write your desire on a slip of paper and burn it or light a candle and visualise – it really can be that simple. But it is interesting to add in all the other bits and bobs as you gain experience. Spell making is personal and you will need to find out what works best for you.

Once you have all your items prepared you need to decide whether to cast a circle or not or whether you want to perform a whole ritual – the choice is yours.

When you are ready to perform the spell take it slowly and carefully and be guided by your intuition. It doesn't matter if you stumble over the words in the chant or spill herbs on the table – hey, it happens! Keep going and follow your spell to the end.

Once you have finished with your spell work, don't forget to ground. You will have raised and worked with a lot of energy and you don't want to hang on to it, let it go. Otherwise you may find you are incredibly tense and on edge and it can give you a heck of a headache. Work with a tree grounding exercise, visualising you are a tree sending your roots down to the earth and allowing the excess energy to flow through the roots into the earth. Or you can place your hands palms down onto the floor and release the energy back into Mother Earth. And of course, you can always eat something to ground; cake and chocolate are the obvious choices.

Note: My advice to you is never to cast a spell when you are angry, tired or feeling poorly ... the magic will definitely go squiffy.

Types of spell

Not all spells need to be cast in a ritual circle with the quarters called and deities invoked, it just depends how much energy and time you want to put into your spell. As a Kitchen Witch, I like to keep it simple. But as always, the choice is yours, if you want to perform a full ritual around your spell, go for it. Alternatively you could just visualise a protective circle of light, or if, like me you feel your house and sacred space are already cleansed and protected you don't need to work a ritual.

Candle spells

This is one of my favourite ways to work magic. For a basic candle spell, you raise energy and push it, together with your intent into the candle, then as the candle burns your energy is released and your intent is taken into the air by the candle smoke. You can also tie some colour magic into your spell by using a corresponding coloured candle.

Using herbs for candle magic is simple and easy. You can anoint the candle with essential oil first and then roll the candle in dried herbs or you can sprinkle the dried herbs on the top of the candle (this works well with tea lights). If I sprinkle the herbs on top of a pillar candle I like to then seal it by dripping candle wax from another candle over the top of the herbs.

Anointing your candle with essential oils adds to the power of your intent and aligns them with your energy. You can also use magic powders on your candles too. If you use the rolled beeswax candles, you can carefully unroll the beeswax sheet and sprinkle herbs or magic powder onto it and roll it back up again.

Decide on your intent; select the candle you wish to use and then use corresponding herbs and oils whose magical properties align with your magical intent.

You can make up batches of dressing oils very easily. Use a base oil such as almond or sunflower oil and add your essential oils and herbs to it.

Basic dressing oil recipe:
3 fluid ounces base oil
12 drops essential oil
1 teaspoon dried herbs

You can even add small crystal chips to the bottle too or a sprig of herb.

Visualisation/Meditation is another simple method and can be used on its own or in combination with other methods, but this should always be included in your spell. For this to work you simply visualise your intent playing out the way you would wish it to.

Medicine bags/mojo bags: You could make a medicine bag which contains items that are symbolic to the intent of your spell. This might contain crystals and herbs that support your need, some of your hair to represent you etc. You make the bag whilst visualising your intent coming to fruition. Medicine bags work well because you can add layers of magic by corresponding the colour of the bag with the crystals and the herbs to your intent, each adding another boost of power. Bags can also be fed regularly with magic/sachet powder to keep the magic 'alive'.

Magic/Sachet powder

Although magic powders also have lots of other uses. They can be used to roll candles in for spell work, to sprinkle around your house for protection, to add oomph to rituals and any spells, to add to poppets and witch bottles or to wear in a small bottle as a charm. The magic powder (called a sachet powder in Hoodoo) is used to 'feed' the energy within your medicine pouch and keep the magic working.

To make a magic powder the ingredients you use must be ground so you will need either a pestle and mortar or the end of a rolling pin and a solid bowl.

As you add each ingredient to the bowl charge it first with your intent. I also like to charge the powder as a whole once it is complete too.

This can then be fed to your medicine bag each week, just a sprinkle; you can even boost the power by feeding it on the corresponding day of the week to your intent.

I like to use a base for my magic powders, I usually use either salt or sugar, and it grinds well and adds its own qualities to the mix too. If I am making faery wishes powder I also like to add in a little bit of glitter (who doesn't?). What else you add is up to you but make sure it is easy to grind to a powder. Dried herbs and spices all work well. Use a suitable chant as you grind the powder together with your intent.

Food magic: Work your spell into whatever baking or cooking you are doing. Or you can bake cookies, a cake or bread with the specific intent in mind and these are also useful in ritual for the feast. Add in a corresponding herb or spice and you also boost the magic for your intent.

Fetish: Creating a magical item from natural things such as bones, feathers and pebbles.

The word 'fetish' possibly originates from a Portuguese word 'feitico' meaning charm or sorcery so essentially it is an item filled with magic and you will find versions of them in most cultures.

A fetish can be an object that has a connection to the supernatural with the item representing the divine or spirit world or some have a spirit that resides within the fetish. Other fetishes are natural objects or any items that have been imbued with magical intent. A fetish is designed and carried or worn to bring protection, love, prosperity or luck and to protect against evil whilst some are created to bring curses upon your enemies.

A fetish can be anything such as a poppet, carved images, animal bones, an ornament or a pouch filled with herbs and other more unsavoury ingredients (think bodily fluids ...). I usually like to use feathers, leaves, twigs and stones as types of fetish. Making your own fetish is advisable (rather than buying one) it will have more power and be personal to you but it doesn't have to be complicated, it can just be a pebble.

Your fetish will need to be activated and by that, I mean you will need to charge it with your magical intent or the energy of the deity or spirit that you want it to have. Sometimes if it is a natural item it may need activating to release the energy of the spirit that is already within it. (Every natural item has its own spirit energy.) Once your fetish is set up it is essentially a 'living thing' and will need attention and even feeding.

You can soak your item in oils or scented water, pass it through incense smoke or add corresponding herbs and if you are dedicating it to a deity use items which are associated with them.

Get creative ... bones, paintings, images, spirit bottles, witches bottles, witches ladders, statues, dolls, poppets, beaded cloth, pebbles, twigs, feathers ... the material choice is endless. All the time you pay your fetish attention and keep feeding the energy it will keep working for you.

Amulets, Talismans & Charms: Tying a spell into a piece of jewellery or crystal. There is always confusion over the meaning for each of these, believe me I get confused too. It is all about attracting and deflecting ...

Talisman – a magically charged object that ATTRACTS a desired energy. Talismans bring power and energy to the wearer. They can be made of anything from natural objects to pieces of parchment inscribed with symbols. You may have a piece of jewellery or an item of clothing which you wear to give you confidence or for luck, this is a talisman.

Amulet – a magically charged object which DEFLECTS unwanted energy. Amulets have been used for protection for thousands of years to protect people's homes, crops and livestock. Originally they would probably have been made using natural objects like stones, animal bones and teeth. Now we can use all sorts of different materials and items. Even a knot in a piece of string could be used as an amulet as the knot will trap the unwanted energy and keep us safe.

If you are creating a talisman for luck you could create it during a waxing moon to enhance the attraction magic, you might use the colour green if you see that as a lucky colour. If it is a natural object like a pebble you might want to draw a four-leaf clover or a similar symbol on it. You get the idea; layer your correspondences to make it as meaningful as possible.

The same rules apply to an amulet; you would create this on a waning moon if possible. Your amulet may be a black gemstone for protection and you might burn sage to cleanse negative energies and put it through the flame of a black candle during its creation.

You will need to charge both the talisman and the amulet with your intent.

Charms – It's a common misconception that a charm is a magical object but in fact it is the words spoken to enchant the object that are the actual charm. The word 'charm' probably originates from either the Latin *carmen* which means incantation, song, lamentation or the French *charme* which means song. But words are flighty 'lil beggars and not believed to hold the same staying power as an actual object and so lucky charms and bags came to be.

When I think of a charm I think of a charm bracelet, an excellent way to wear and have several different charms at once. Or maybe a horseshoe that hangs outside your door for luck. A charm is nearly always to bring good fortune your way, hence the term 'lucky charm'.

Container spells: Witch bottles, poppets, jar and box spells. This kind of spell is probably self-explanatory – it is a spell in a container whether it is a jar, a bottle, a box or a poppet.

Witch bottles

I love using witch bottles, I always have two on the go in my house for protection, clearing out negative energies and bringing happiness to the home. These are so easy to make, you don't need special pretty bottles you can just use old, clean jam jars.

In general terms, the witch bottles we make today are very similar to witch bottles found centuries ago, the structure is the same but the intent differs quite a lot. Originally it was believed witch bottles were created to protect against witches … They also used to contain all sorts of bodily fluids, hair and finger nail clippings – you can still use these if you wish.

Basically, a witch bottle is a container of some sort, usually a jar or a bottle, which is filled with objects corresponding with and charged with a specific magical intent.

The typical contents of the basic protective witch bottle today are quite similar to that of the traditional one: nails, sand, crystals, stones, knotted threads, herbs, spices, resin, flowers, candle wax, incense, salt, vinegar, oil, coins, saw dust, ashes etc., etc. Everything used in a standard spell can be used in this bottled version.

Start with your jar or bottle, then charge each item before you add it, layering up the 'ingredients' as you go.

It really is up to you what you put in. I like to put in three nails to draw any negative energy out of the house and into the bottle for protection. I also put in a piece of string with three knots, knotting in my intent with each tie. If it is for prosperity I often drop in a silver coin. I usually put salt in for protection, cleansing and purification. I also like to add a variety of dried pulse – lentils or beans to 'soak' up any negative energies. Garlic is good for protection too. Then add any herbs, spices and flowers that correspond with your intent – rose petals for love, cinnamon for success, mint and basil for prosperity etc. Keep filling the jar or bottle up until you reach the top then put the lid on. If you are using a jam jar, I like to draw a pentacle on the lid. If I am using a bottle with a cork, I like to seal the cork lid with dripped wax, not for any other reason except that it looks fabulous ...

If you are making the witch bottle for protection for your own home I like to put in a pebble from the garden, a couple of fallen leaves from the tree in my yard and a bit of cobweb from inside the house, it makes it all more personal and ties the bottle to the energies of the home.

Money jar

A twist on the witches' bottle is a money jar.

Use a clean, cleansed jar and half fill it with rice or seeds (fenugreek seeds are good). As you half fill the jar visualise prosperity and abundance. Then every day add two more seeds to the jar, visualising prosperity as you do. When the jar is full bury it whilst sending up a request to deity that your desire be fulfilled.

You can also do this with a jar and your loose change, each time you drop a couple of coins in the jar visualise prosperity, every so often sprinkle in a few herbs that correspond with prosperity such as basil or mint. When the jar is full you can count it up and use it for something special.

Honey jar spells

This is a very traditional type of bottle spell. It is essentially a jar that has a sweet liquid inside, you then add your magical ingredients such as connections to the person if you are directing it towards an individual, herbs and maybe a written charm on a piece of paper. This is all topped off by dressing a candle with a corresponding essential oil and then the candle is burnt on top of the jar. You can use a honey or a syrup jar for this working. Honey is excellent to 'make life sweet' or to bring something or someone together. It also brings the magical energy of happiness, healing, love, prosperity, passion and spirituality – lots to choose from.

Vinegar jar spells

Pickle or chutney jars work well for any kind of protection or fire magic. Once the contents have been eaten, keep the remaining vinegar in the jar and add extra items of your choosing to it.

Shaking bottle spells

Shaking a bottle spell once you have set the magic gives it a bit of a stir up, gets the energy within the spell working and adds an extra oomph to it. If you keep the bottle spell for an ongoing working you can regularly shake it to keep the energy flowing.

Be creative, even an empty tomato sauce bottle would work as tomato brings love, passion, protection and creativity.

Don't stop with jars or bottles ... what about tins? Once you have emptied the contents into your recipe you could use the tin for magical workings (not so easy to seal though).

Poppets

When most people think of a poppet, they automatically think of the Voodoo doll, thanks to this item's negative portrayal in movies and on television. However, the use of dolls in sympathetic magic goes back several millennia. Back in the days of ancient Egypt, the enemies of Ramses III (he had a lot) used wax images of the Pharaoh, to bring about his death. Greek poppets called Kolossoi were sometimes used to restrain a ghost or even a dangerous deity, or to bind two lovers together.

I like to think of a poppet as a person-shaped spell holder and use them for love, luck, protection, prosperity and healing.

Remember that poppets have a long tradition behind them, and that tradition is influenced by the magical practices of a wide range of cultures. Treat your poppets well, and they will do the same for you.

As for design, well it's up to you. You can make a simple poppet from twine, grasses or ivy tied together right up to detailed material poppets with hair and glass eyes and of course anywhere in between. You can even use dollies, Barbie dolls or a potato.

I like to use felt when making poppets because I hate sewing. With felt you don't have to hem. And of course, felt comes in all sorts of colours so you can correspond the colour of felt used to the intent.

I cut out two felt shapes, a bit like a gingerbread man or a 'T' shape. Then I sew one button on for one eye and a cross for the other eye, followed by a mouth. Then I sew on a little red felt heart.

Next, I sew with neat but not fancy stitches around the edges of the figure, again you can use coloured thread to correspond with your intent.

I leave a gap and then stuff the poppet with some off-cuts of felt but also herbs and spices; occasionally I will add a crystal too. You can use all sorts of herbs, woods, plants, roots and spices even salt and rice – go with what suits your intent or what feels right for you. Salt, rice and dried pulses are good if your poppet is larger as they fill up the space nicely and work for purification, protection, negative energy and in the case of rice, prosperity too. Charge each item as you add it. Then when your poppet is full sew it up. I like to charge it with my intent again once completed.

I like to set the poppet on my altar and recharge him occasionally with my intent. Some people choose to bury the poppet once it is made, allowing the universe to work the magic, the choice is yours.

Witches' ladders

The first recorded find of a witches' ladder was in 1886 during the repairs of an old house in Somerset, England. Within the roof space they found a pile of broomsticks, an old chair and a length of braided cord, with a loop at one end and lots of cockerel feathers threaded through the braid.

Over the years there have been many theories as to the purpose of the braid but the most popular seems to be that the ladder was for cursing. With ideas ranging from curdling the milk from a neighbour's cow through to wishing someone dead. Other ideas suggest that it was used for healing or casting wishes. The fact is that nobody really knows …

The witch ladder is one of my favourite magical tools and they are seen nowadays in many forms but all usually with the basic braid of three cords together with feathers in between, often nine of them. I also like to add sprigs of herbs to mine and a bit of colour magic in the form of ribbons.

Making a witch ladder

Cut nine pieces of natural twine or ribbon (or a mixture of both), about 1 metre in length.

If you are going to use ribbon then think about colour too. Pick the colour to match the intent of your witch ladder. Gather together three strands and tie a knot in one end, then begin to plait together tying a knot at the other end when you have finished. Repeat with the other strands until you have three sets of three plaited lengths. Then you are going to plait these together. While you are working focus on your intent, maybe even chant as you go.

If you are crafty you can add in beads, charms or other embellishments. Or if you are like me, sew them on afterwards. Once you have your completed plait, make sure it is secure at both ends. Then at regular intervals poke in a feather or piece of herb between the braiding. As you do this focus on the intent.

Place your finished witch ladder on your altar or put it someone where you will see it every day until your purpose has come to fruition. The intent can be whatever you want or need it to be – love, healing, protection, prosperity. The options are limitless.

Cord magic

Cord magic is essentially just that – magic using a cord. Often the cord is plaited/braided together and it can be made from cord, twine, string, ribbon, fabric or even natural items such as long grasses. Witch ladders are a sort of cord magic. The cord can be created and hung up above your altar, your bed or above a doorway or it can be created for a personal intent and worn. Larger cords can be used as belts or smaller ones worn as bracelets. You weave your intent into the cord as you braid it. Cords can also be created to honour specific deities.

Cords can be used to create a circle too, especially useful if you are away from home and need to create a sacred space.

Colour magic can be brought in and the intent of the spell reflected in the colour of the cord or ribbons used.

Knot magic

Leading on from cord magic is working with a cord that you tie knots in. You work your intent into each knot as you tie it. Other items can also be added such as hair or sprigs of herbs that you tie into the centre of each knot.

There is a traditional chant used for knot magic:

By the knot of one, the spell has begun
By the knot of two, it will come true
By the knot of three, so shall it be
By the knot of four, it is strengthened more
By the knot of five, so may it thrive
By the knot of six, this spell is fixed
By the knot of seven, be it powered by the heavens
By the knot of eight, guide the hand of fate
By the knot of nine, the thing is mine

The cord can then be put in a safe place or carried with you.

You can use knot magic to prepare a spell ahead of time, for instance if you want to capture the energy of a new moon to use later. You would 'tie' the energy on a new moon night into a cord using knots. Then when you want to use new moon energy later you untie each knot to release the power. Traditionally you would tie nine knots all on one day but release them over a period of nine days, one each day. On the ninth day, the final knot releases the biggest boost of power. The length of cord used is often nine feet which is three times three – a magical number, but that is a large piece of cord to use and work with so go with a length that works for you.

Basically, the knot is a container for the magical energy; once you untie it the energy is released. It can be used for all sorts of intents such as healing or to bind in pain but they can also be used in binding spells.

Crystal spells

Crystals have long been believed to hold magical powers. Although I don't believe they were used in folk magic very much they are extremely popular today. Each crystal has its own unique and individual magical property and that can be tapped into for your spell work. Whether you just sit and hold a crystal and visualise your desire or place crystals around the home or workplace to bring positive energy in or take negative energy out, they are extremely useful. I often place crystals at the base of a candle when I am working with candle magic or add small crystals to medicine pouches and witch bottles.

Another favourite of mine is to work with crystal grids, these can be any size you want (also dependent on how many crystals you own) even a small grid of four or five crystals will work well. I also like to add in feathers, pebbles, shells, herbs and tarot/oracle cards to my crystal grids.

A crystal grid is a geometric pattern of crystals, each one charged with intent and adding its own power to the other crystals in the grid.

First, you need to decide what your intent is for creating the grid. They can be created for just about any purpose. Make sure your intent is clear and specific because you don't want the 'power' wandering off in unspecified directions …

You can draw out a sacred geometry pattern to work from or print one from the net, but I prefer to work intuitively, whatever way works best for you. A hexagon is a decent shape to start with but you can also use triangles, squares, circles, stars, a spiral or the infinity symbol.

I start with the centre stone; this creates the key point or the power stone. This stone is the amplifier or the connector for the whole grid. I like to use a larger crystal as the centre stone, whilst this isn't essential it does seem to 'conduct' the power more efficiently.

Don't feel you can't create a crystal grid if you can't afford to buy a big crystal, even if you only have a small selection of tumble stones you can still create an effective grid.

How many surrounding stones you use is up to you and the size of grid you want to create. I also like to charge each stone with the intent as I place it. Start with a basic design and see where your intuition takes you – there is no right or wrong.

To choose the crystals for your grid, go with your instinct or look up the meanings or even just work with the colour that you feel is right for your intent. You can also add other items into the grid such as business cards, photos or items of jewellery. You can add more than one 'ring' of stones around your centre stone, each new layer will increase and amplify energies. Go with your intuition, what stones you have and the amount of space you have to work with. I recommend you put your grid in a safe place where it won't be disturbed by pets or small children. You may only feel that the grid needs to be left up for an hour or two, but you might want to leave it in place for days or weeks – getting everyone to step around a 4-foot crystal grid in the centre of the living room probably isn't practical … You might like to light candles and incense as you create the grid as well.

Once your grid is all set up you need to activate it. Some people like to use a specific crystal or metal wand to activate each stone in the grid, personally I just use a quartz crystal point, but the choice is yours as to what you use (and what you can afford) a well-aimed finger works just as well. Once you are all set up take a moment to calm and centre yourself, then say out loud your intent, it might just be a statement, an affirmation or, if you are poetic, you could say it in verse.

As you state your intent point your activation wand/crystal or your finger at the centre stone and visualise energy coming up from the earth (or down from the sky) through your body, down your arm and out through your hand into the centre crystal (you don't need to make actual contact with the crystal) then move your wand from crystal to crystal around the grid linking the energy beam from one stone to the next repeating your intent as you go.

Once you have linked all the stones take an overall look at the grid and visualise your required outcome. Then ground yourself and let the grid do its work. You should instinctively know when the grid is done and when you can dismantle it or you may feel that it needs longer and requires recharging later, if it needs recharging just repeat the activation sequence again. Don't ignore your grid, I am not suggesting it will need recharging every day but take some time every few days just to take notice of it and re-visualise your intent.

If you chose to place other items in your grid they will charge nicely with the energy and in the case of jewellery, these can be taken out and worn, thereby carrying the energy from the grid with you.

If you have the room you can create a crystal grid large enough for you to sit in, this is wonderful for re-energising yourself.

When you do take a crystal grid apart don't forget to cleanse all the crystals you used.

Mirror magic

Mirrors have a bit of a reputation in fairy tales and folk stories but mirrors or reflective surfaces have long been used for magical purposes, often as part of a spell, for meditation or for divination. Anything reflective can work as a mirror including surfaces of the water, glass, polished stones, shiny plastic, silver and metal and pieces of aluminium foil. The main feature of a mirror is: it reflects (this can be used in spell work for reflecting on what is to come or what has been); as a gateway to the Otherworld; protection and shielding; seeing the truth; reflecting your true inner self or, of course, reflecting negative energy and curses back to the sender.

I keep a jar of broken pieces of mirror and glass in my magical store cupboard to use in spell work.

Petition papers

Petition papers and name papers are slips of paper that you write a person's name on or a symbol or sigil or short phrase corresponding with the intent of your spell work. Mostly, the petition papers and name papers are placed under a candle, added to a mojo bag or bottle. Name papers will have a person's name on, the intended recipient of the spell, whilst a petition paper will have a wish or desire.

You can add to the oomph of the spell by using coloured ink to write on your paper, so for instance black ink for protection and reversing spells, or green ink for money spells. In traditional hoodoo practice only red or black ink would be used, and often it would be dove blood, dragon blood or bat blood ink. You can use real blood but please don't kill animals just to use their blood in magic. You could ask at your local butcher shop, although I think they might struggle to supply dragon blood, but you never know … Dragon blood ink can be created by putting a few drops of dragon blood (which is actually tree resin) essential oil into coloured ink.

What paper you use is up to you, you can tear a small piece from a brown paper bag or a sheet of printer paper or you could use handmade parchment. Using paper with torn edges allows the magic to seep out.

Use scissors for banishing petitions or for cutting ties with someone or something.

As a general guide for using petition papers you would write the person's name or your wish on the slip of paper three times, then turn the paper ninety degrees clockwise and write the name or wish again three times over the top of the first ones. The petition paper should then be dressed with a suitable oil blend.

The petition paper is then folded, to draw things to you the paper should be folded towards you, to banish something fold the paper away from you, either way keep folding the paper until you can fold it no more.

The petition paper can then be placed under a candle or in a mojo bag or a bottle.

Sigils

Sigil magic is very easy to work and requires very few items – just paper and a pen or even a handful of salt to draw the sigil on the ground with. Simply put, a sigil is a symbol that is drawn to represent a specific desire or goal that you would like to manifest into your life. They are a point to help focus magical energy for your intent.

Start by sitting quietly, somewhere that you won't be distracted or disturbed. If you prefer you can create a sacred circle and/or light a candle and some incense to help you focus. Clear your mind as well as you can then focus on your intent.

Write down your goal or desire onto the piece of paper but only use one sentence to sum it up. *Be specific*. So, I might write "This book will be a huge success" (well, every little helps, doesn't it?). Keep the words positive and succinct. Next you need to strike out the vowels from the sentence, so mine would look like this:

Thsbkwllbhgsccss

Then remove any duplicate letters, mine would then look like this:

Thsbkwlgc

Now for the interesting part; you need to create a design using just the remaining letters. Write them out in a spiral, a square, over the top of each other – it doesn't matter how. Be guided by your intuition and create a pleasing image with them. Don't stress too much over it, allow your mind to wander and your pen to doodle.

The finished design will be your very own sigil. Now you need to activate the magic. The best way to do this is to burn the paper with the sigil drawn on it. Light the corner of the paper on a candle flame and drop it into a cauldron. The magic is activated and released. You could also drop the paper into running water or bury it, but I find that the latter methods produce slower results. Experiment and see what works for you.

Here are three different options for my sigil using the letters above:

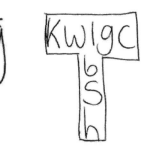

Tarot spells

Using tarot cards or oracle cards in your spell gives you a focal point and helps with visualisation. They can be used as a signifier for a person i.e. the person you are sending healing to (or a curse). They can also bring the power and energy of the card itself. For instance, the 'lovers' card could be used in a love spell to signify the couple but also in a spell for a decision to choose between two different pathways. You can use your normal tarot set for spell work but I prefer a separate deck that I use just for spells. Sometimes the card needs to sit in the spell for a day or even a few days and I don't want to be doing tarot readings with cards missing.

Here are some suggested cards to use in spell work and their correspondences:

Action/to set things in motion: The Chariot, Ace of Wands,

Eight of Wands.

To overcome a bad habit: Strength, Temperance, Judgement, The World.

For inspiration, ideas and creativity: The Magician, The Moon, The Star.

New business/project success: The Magician, The Sun, Ace of Wands.

Business prosperity: Three of Wands, The Sun, Ace of Pentacles.

To bring about change: Wheel of Fortune, The Magician, Eight of Wands, Judgement.

Fertility: The Sun, Ten of Cups, Ace of Wands.

For success: The Chariot, Six of Wands, Five of Wands.

For courage: The Star, Strength, The Chariot.

To help with a decision: Justice, The Hermit, The Star, The Lovers.

For dream work: The Star, The Moon, Ace of Cups, High Priestess.

Happiness and positive energy: The Sun, The World, Ace of Cups.

To release guilt and pain: The Moon, Judgement, The World.

For binding spells: Temperance, Two of Swords, Eight of Swords, Hanged Man.

Friendship: Three of Cups, Two of Cups, Knight of Cups.

Healing and good health: Strength, The World, The Magician, The Sun, The Star, Three of Cups.

For employment: Eight of Pentacles, The Emperor, Judgement, Page of Wands.

For knowledge: The Hermit, High Priestess, The Moon.

For love: The Lovers, Knight of Cups, The Star.

Luck: The World, The Star, Wheel of Fortune.

Prosperity and money: Ten of Pentacles, Knight of Pentacles, Page of Pentacles, Six of Pentacles, Ace of Pentacles.

Overcoming obstacles: Two of Cups, The Chariot, Strength.

For protection: The Star, The Chariot, Temperance, Four of Wands.

Self-improvement and transformation: Temperance, The World, Judgement, The Magician, Strength, High Priestess, The Chariot.

Stress relief: Hanged Man, Ace of Cups, Temperance, Four of Cups.

People in spells

Some spells will require a representation of either yourself or the recipient of the magic. What you use is up to you. Photographs work well because there is no doubt who the person is from the image but you don't always have access to a photograph. A piece of their hair, toe nail clipping (if you don't know the person well enough to have a photograph of them I don't want to know how you managed to get one of their toe nail clippings …) or a drop of blood works. If using bodily fluids is your thing then menstrual blood, saliva, sweat, urine or sexual fluids can be used very effectively. It is probably easier to get the personal body items if you are working magic for yourself or a family member. You can also use something that reminds you of the person, such as their favourite flower or a piece of jewellery. Tarot cards can be used as signifiers for specific people, a card that echoes their personality. Even a 'person shaped' potato will do. If you know categorically that it represents that person, pretty much anything can be used.

Sympathetic magic

This is a term that is often used and one which I wanted to include to cover the meaning.

The dictionary says:

Primitive or magical ritual using objects or actions resembling or symbolically associated with the event or person over which influence is sought.

Every time we use a corresponding herb or colour we are using sympathetic magic because of the associations. We use the colour red in magical spells for passion and love because we associate the colour red with those emotions.

The poppet is a fine example of sympathetic magic as we use it to represent a person within the spell working.

Curses, hexes and bindings

Knowledge is power. If you know about curses and hexes then you are fore-warned and fore-armed. If you choose to hex or curse then that of course is your right to do so, just be mindful of the backlash ...

I am also not going to get on a soap box and spout off about morals, taking the high ground, karma etc., – that choice is yours to make, and yours alone.

My personal thoughts are: if you get cross or upset about something or with someone; stop and think. Don't just blindly work a spell to curse or hex someone in the heat of anger. Let the hurt die down first, and then decide what course of action to take.

Sometimes there are situations that warrant action or reaction and sometimes it is not easy to decide what course to follow. A good rule of thumb to follow is if you would not do it in reality then don't do it with magic. Make sure that what you do, whatever kind of defensive action you take is equivalent to the action that was taken against you. You would not blow up someone's car just for stepping on your toe, would you? Think about your plan of action, if you feel uncomfortable in any way then don't do it, go back to the drawing board and come up with Plan B, C or D (and all the rest of the letters in the alphabet if need be).

Curses and hexes are not for the faint hearted and if you decide that is the path you want to go down, I urge you to not take them lightly and never chuck them about willy nilly – take responsibility for your actions. You also need to be very, very sure that the person you are sending a curse or hex to is the person responsible ...

Okay, so let's look at what hexes and curses are.

Just as there are hundreds and thousands of love and prosperity spells there are probably just as many hexes. Some of them involve long complicated rituals, some require all sorts of ingredients and others are just gestures with a hand or a word.

So, what is the difference between a hex and a curse? Well I am not sure there is much of a difference to be honest, just different names from diverse cultures. However, the consensus seems to be that a hex is a spell or bewitchment, traditionally they could be good or bad and a witch could be paid to provide one. A curse is a malevolent spell that is cast with the purpose of inflicting harm upon another; curses can be spoken or written. Objects can also be cursed with bad luck, misfortune, ill health and even death.

Essentially it's the wilful direction of negative energy towards someone with the intent to harm. Usually hexes and curses take some time to develop, building up slowly. However, if you are well shielded and protected you are very unlikely to become the victim of a hex yourself and I think it happens a lot less frequently than people believe.

Binding

I would also like to look at binding; this is a form of spell that binds a person or situation so that they/it can no longer harm you. I have found this form of working particularly successful, if you are pure in your intent, it doesn't harm the person or cause them any discomfort it just stops them from hurting or harassing you. Bear in mind that this spell does take away the free will of the person you are binding, so use with caution.

A binding spell can be very simple – you use an object that represents the person causing you harm – it can be a poppet, it could be a photograph or it could just be a lump of clay that you have identified as the person. It can then be bound, with string, ribbon or even sticky tape. As you bind the object visualise binding the harmful energies of that person and speak your wishes, that the person can no longer harm you or harass you. Bury the spell.

Banishing

On to banishing, now, I have had a lot of experience with this and not all of it has been good. I thought it sounded like a lovely idea to 'banish negative energy' from my life. What I didn't expect was the huge circle that this type of banishing covers. It does not just get rid of bad luck, it covers all sorts of things ... including people. To banish all negative energy from your life is not always a good thing. We all need balance in life, for instance think about batteries – they need positive and negative to work – and if you took away the negative they would have no power.

Much better to ask that "any negative energy that serves me no good be released", it's safer believe me! Note I used the word 'release' rather than 'banish', I have found it is safer. But please be prepared for unexpected results ...

A very simple banishing spell is to use some slips of paper and a cauldron. Write what you want to banish on the slips of paper, light the corner of each slip on a candle and drop it into the cauldron, visualising the feeling/emotion/bad habit/ whatever disappearing. Send the ashes out into the wind or into running water (or even down the toilet).

Another simple idea is to write what you want to be rid of on a slip of paper and drop it into running water or again even to flush it down the toilet.

PLEASE remember that whatever you banish leaves a hole, that hole must be purposely filled with positive energy otherwise it will just be replaced with that which is similar to what you wanted to get rid of in the first place. I find it wise to add onto the end of a banishing something like "and fill the void with love and blessings".

And remember that banishings sometimes take some time to work too.

Exploding spells: A cautionary tale

Every new moon I work some magic usually in the form of writing a cheque to myself from the universe. Occasionally I feel inspired to work some candle magic too which is what happened recently. I did my usual cheque-writing and then set about creating a candle magic spell for new opportunities, success and prosperity.

My candle magic is usually set in a ceramic dish I have specifically for that purpose. It has a central dish with a 'moat' around the edge. Basically, it is a small 'chip n dip' dish but it works perfectly for putting a candle in the centre and surrounding it with herbs, crystals or magical ingredients.

I like to keep things simple, so I started with a gold candle in the centre which I sprinkled with dried lemon balm. Around the edge in the 'moat' I put cinnamon bark, dried beans and popped lotus seeds.

I lit the candle and sat back to watch the flame. I never leave a candle unattended; sometimes I might be doing other things in the same room, I do keep an eye on it. However, on this occasion I was drawn to sit and watch.

Thankfully I did because once the candle had burnt down to the end and was just a flame eating up the last remnants of wax that had melted onto the base … there was an almighty loud 'CRACK' followed by herbs and beans flying across the altar and the dish split in two. Flames were now taking hold of the velvet cloth underneath and quickly made a start on the varnish of the sideboard beneath.

I blew out the flames as fast as I could but everything was too hot to handle so I had to run and get a pair of tongs from the kitchen to pick up the embers to stop it spreading.

The outcome was a melted hole in the velvet cloth and a scorch mark on the sideboard and of course a ceramic dish that is now in two pieces. If I had been in another room I dread to think what would have happened as there were plenty of flammable items on my altar including the altar itself and above it several shelves of books.

It was a harsh reminder that flames should not be left alone and perhaps also that new moon energy can be powerful.

Remember your manners

On the last full moon, I worked some candle magic for prosperity, nothing fancy just a gold candle, a few herbs and heap loads of intent. This week the spell was fulfilled just when it was needed.

I wanted to thank the gods, literally.

Having recently moved my office around in our house, my main altar hadn't been put back up properly although I have had a small altar to Ganesha on my desk to celebrate Ganesha Chaturthi (his 10-day birthday celebration).

So, the altar was where I started, giving it a good clean and clear out and relaying clean, new and fresh items along with herbs and flowers from the garden.

Dressing your altar and leaving offerings of food and flowers is an excellent way to say thank you when the gods have come through for you.

The garden also got a bit of a tidy and I fed the birds, although I do that most days anyway, but dead heading, tidying plants and bird feeding is also an effective way to say thank you to Mother Nature herself. I have also placed fresh flowers in the vase by my Lakshmi image and honey for Ganesha – these two remove obstacles and allow the abundance to flow. I like them lots.

As the wheel is turning it is time for my matron goddess the Cailleach to show herself too, so a lot of my freshly set out altar is to welcome her back.

When I have worked spells I like to give thanks on their fruition, it is after all only good manners. And if I keep asking the gods for favours and giving nothing in return I am pretty sure they would get fed up with my requests quickly.

Just remember to say thank you …

My thoughts on love spells

I get an awful lot of queries via email, message and in the Kitchen Witch Facebook group about love spells. So here are my thoughts. This is my humble opinion, you don't have to take on board what I think and it is a little bit of a rant …

We get variations on a theme but here are the two main scenarios:

Situation one:

My husband has left me and moved in with another woman. He would not have done that on his own so I believe the other woman has put a spell on him. I want to cast a spell that will bring him back.

Okay, you know what? Sometimes life sucks and this happens, there is usually no occult connection at all and the 'other woman' is not a witch/druid/wizard/sorcerer/root worker or even remotely spiritual or magical. Firstly, I am not sure I would want a man back who had left me for another woman but maybe that's just me. Secondly, have you spoken to your husband? Have you asked him why? Does his explanation seem reasonable? Maybe the husband had a good reason to leave or maybe it was just one of those life experiences that happen.

Situation two:

My wife has left me and our children and I want her back, she should be here in the home being a wife and mother. I want a spell to bring her back.

Well ... I wonder why she left? How do we know that the husband is a good husband? Maybe she left because she fell out of love (it happens), maybe she left because he was horrible! We just don't know. And any spell to bring her back would be working against her own free will, what right have you got to demand she return? Have you spoken to her? Have you tried to win her back with love, affection and attention? Have you asked her why she left?

The trouble is with most of these situations we don't know all the details and we never get both sides of the story and even if we did what business is it of ours and who can guarantee that what someone says is the truth?

Why do people think the solution is to just throw a spell at it? Relationships are hard work, they take time and effort and if you don't put that into it then things go wrong. Heck, things go wrong in relationships anyway, that's life. It isn't a bed of roses (which is a strange phrase as lying on a bed of roses would be very uncomfortable me thinks). Do the work ... see what you can do to resolve the issues but sometimes it just happens and there isn't a thing you can do about it but deal with the situation as best you can and move on with your life.

The other scenario is being asked for a love spell to attract a soul mate, often this is for someone specific and I must say ... this can only end badly. Back to free will here ... Do you really want to cast a spell and have the man/woman of your desire go out with you purely on the strength of a spell? Wouldn't you rather know that someone was with you because they truly liked you?

Love spells are useful for drawing a soul mate if you aren't particularly targeting a specific person, in fact they work very well if you want to spice up your current love life or keep fidelity in your relationship. When you want to write that love spell to attract someone to you I would recommend you really leave it loosely worded and up to the universe, it usually knows best because what we want isn't always what we need.

Think about this ...

If you ask specifically for someone with a good sense of humour you may get someone who treats life as a complete joke ... the whole time.

If you ask specifically for someone to treat you like a lady you may end up with someone who expects you to do all the housework, cleaning, tidying, washing, ironing and have their dinner on the table at night.

If you ask specifically for someone wealthy you may get it but you may also end up with someone who works all the hours under the sun and never has time for you.

Do you see where I am going with this?

Just think carefully about it.

Spells have a habit of going off in unexpected directions ...

Love is special. Love is wonderful when it works, and relationships when they are tended and fed can be amazing. But it all takes work, not the 'light a candle and throw some herbs at it' kind of work but the real time, effort, communication, trust and spending time together kind of work.

However, having said that we can all use a little bit of help occasionally and love spells to rejuvenate a relationship or to bring love to you can work very effectively. I have included some love spell suggestions further on in the book – how or if you use them is up to you.

Sex magic

Energy can be raised in the obvious sexual manner i.e. climax of orgasm, and this can be used to direct the energy and intent to a spell. It can be worked alone or as a couple but in my own humble opinion sex magic works best between a couple that love each other; never in front of an 'audience'. If you are ever part of a coven that asks you to have sex in ritual and you feel uncomfortable with it – walk away. NEVER be pressured into doing something that doesn't feel right to you.

Casual sex has a different energy to it and none of the spiritual connections. There are or have been more so in the past, groups on the edges of the occult that have used magic as an excuse for sexual promiscuity. Thankfully they are/were a small minority.

Correspondences

If you want to add oomph to your spell workings then bringing in correspondences will do just that. You don't have to work with all of them because seriously sometimes you can't wait until the correct day of the week or moon phase to happen. Again, trust your intuition.

Think about correspondences, this could include the timing of your spell according to the phases of the moon or day of the week. Which herbs and crystals to use in your charm bag or what colour candle to use. You can get a feel or be guided by lists, my advice with this is to go with your intuition with correspondences; if something doesn't feel right to you then it won't draw the right focus from you. As well as having physical items like candles and herbs that are part of your spell, you may also like to give some thought to items to help set the mood, like incense or the colour of your altar cloth.

Days of the week

If you are organised and can plan ahead, working with the day of the week that corresponds to the type of spell you wish to cast can add power to it.

Monday – Fertility, intuition, emotions, clarity, wisdom, dreams, travel, feminine energy, peace, moon magic and illusions.

Tuesday – Success, strength, defence, protection, courage and challenges.

Wednesday – Communication, fortune, luck, changes, creativity, wild magic, cunning and the arts.

Thursday – Healing, strength, prosperity, wealth, abundance, protection and good health.

Friday – Romance, friendships, passion, fertility and love.

Saturday – Protection, wisdom, spirituality, cleansing and banishing.

Sunday – Prosperity, success, wealth, promotion, fame, personal achievements and acknowledgement.

Times of the day

If you are a busy person like me then the chances are you won't usually be able to work your spells at a specific time of the day. Getting the children ready for school, making the breakfast and showering and dressing yourself whilst trying to summon demons to do your bidding to coincide with the correct time of day is a bit of a push. Go with what works for you, but if you do have the luxury to set your spells into action at a corresponding time of the day give it a try.

Dawn – Renewal, beginnings, rebirth and restoration.

Noon – Energy, power, hopes, dreams, desires, strength, passion and creativity.

Dusk – Inner work, insight, inspiration, planning, adjustments, spirituality and clarity.

Midnight – Spirit work, mysteries, divination, meditation, inner work and candle magic.

Moon phases

Working magic on the corresponding phase of the moon can have a really powerful effect on your spells.

New moon – New beginnings, releasing bad habits, creativity, new projects, planning ventures, house hunting, new jobs, change, stability, positive energy, emotions, business, courage, optimism, luck, prosperity, wishes and growth.

Waxing moon – Healing, energy, activity, friendships, meetings, communication, planning, regeneration, information, positive energy, confidence, patience and protection.

Full moon – Cleansing, purifying, transformations, psychic abilities, divination, strength, love, reconciliations, prosperity, wishes, power and fertility.

Waning moon – Addictions, decisions, divorce, emotions, stress, protection, knowledge, expressions, communication, meditation, clearing, reflection, reversing, banishing and releasing.

Dark moon – Addictions, change, enemies, dreams, obstacles, arguments, removal, separation, love, protection, relationships, inner work and divination.

Blue moon – Work magic on the blue moon (a second full moon in a month) for something that you believe to be unobtainable or difficult to achieve after all it is 'once in a blue moon'.

For more details on working with the moon phases see my book *Pagan Portals: Moon Magic.* (Did you catch that subtle plug?)

Number magic

Saying a chant a certain number of times or adding a specific number of ingredients can all add oomph to your spell working. Each number has magical correspondences. Here are the basic ones but as always, trust your intuition.

1. Strength, purity, unity, action, ideas, independence, courage, determination.
2. Co-operation, adaptability, consideration, spirituality.
3. Trinity, family, inspiration, imagination, creativity, insights, fun.
4. Balance, solidarity, elements, order, growth, details, achievements, organisation.
5. Expansion, creativity, ideas, changes, exploration, promotion, resources, freedom.

6. Marriage, balance, as above/so below, responsibility, community, balance, sympathy, home.
7. Magic, psychic abilities, research, knowledge, meditation, peace, perfection.
8. Leadership, politics, power, authority, work, recognition, judgement, decisions.
9. Inspiration, healing, regeneration, friendship, selflessness, expression, the arts.

Magical alphabets

It can be fun and interesting to write down your spells and petitions in a magical alphabet i.e. not the A-Z variety. There are several that lend themselves to magical work; the one that springs to mind first is the Theban alphabet, often known as the witches' alphabet. But using runes as an alphabet works very well too. Just remember what you have written and how to translate it.

insert image of Theban alphabet

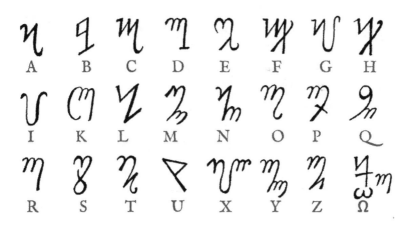

Herbs & Spices

Herbs are the back bone of my magical workings and I grow as many herbs, plants and flowers in my garden as I can physically stuff in there. If you don't have the time or space for gardening you can use store bought herbs, check out your local Asian stores or farmers' markets for the best prices. Supermarket herbs are absolutely fine to use and even out of date ones as well – don't waste anything! These can be sprinkled around your altar or the boundaries of your home, added to witch bottles or medicine pouches and you can roll your candles in them. They can also be ground and made into sachet/magic powders. Hang in bunches over door and window frames – really the magical uses are endless ... You can even eat them.

Here is a very basic list (for more details see my books *A Kitchen Witch's World of Magical Plants & Herbs* and *A Kitchen Witch's World of Magical Food*). Not so subtle plug ...

Lemon Balm – Love, success, healing.

Basil – Love, exorcism, wealth, flying, protection.

Bay – Protection, psychic powers, healing, purification, strength.

Birch – Protection, exorcism, purification.

Camellia – Riches.

Carnation – Protection, strength, healing.

Cinnamon – Spirituality, success, healing, power, psychic powers, lust, protection, love.

Dandelion – Divination, wishes, calling spirits.

Fennel – Protection, healing, purification.

Ivy – Protection, healing.

Lavender – Love, protection, sleep, chastity, longevity, purification, happiness, peace.

Marjoram – Protection, love, happiness, health, money.

Mint – Money, lust, healing, travel, exorcism, protection.

Nettle – Exorcism, protection, healing, lust.

Parsley – Lust, protection, purification.

Poppy – Fertility, love, sleep, money, luck, invisibility.

Rose – Love, psychic powers, healing, love divination, luck, protection.

Rosemary – Protection, love, lust, mental powers, exorcism, purification, healing, sleep.

Sage – Immortality, wishes, longevity, wisdom, protection.

Essential oils

If you want to add a bit more power to your candle spells you can dress the candle with an essential oil or blend of oils corresponding to the intent, before working the spell.

I like to use a base carrier oil such as almond or olive oil, you only need a small amount, 5ml will do. Pop the carrier oil into a small bottle, jar or dish. Then add 2 or 3 drops of your chosen essential oils or oils to create a specific oil blend loaded with your intent. You can correspond the choice of oils to your intent.

Hold the container of oil in your hands and charge it with the energy of your intent. Then dress your candle with the oil blend.

Go with what works for you. You can rub the oil from the bottom of the candle to the centre then down from the top to the centre, bringing the energies together; or if you could work straight down from the top to the bottom to bring energy in; or from the bottom to the top to dispel energy. Be guided by your intuition.

The essential oil blend can be used to dress the candle; then it also provides a sticky base which can be used to roll your candle in dried herbs or spices.

Crystals

I suspect most witches have at least one crystal (and usually quite a lot more), they are like tarot cards – they seem to multiply when you aren't looking. I use crystals mostly for spell work, adding them into medicine pouches and making a circle of crystals around candle spells. I also like to work with crystals in crystal grids and mandalas.

Here is a very basic guideline, but there are an infinite number of diverse types of crystal, go with what works for you or what you have to hand. If you only use one crystal then you can't go wrong with clear quartz for a good 'all-rounder'.

Astral projection – Quartz, opal.

Business success – Bloodstone, malachite, green tourmaline.

Courage – Agate, amethyst, bloodstone, carnelian, lapis lazuli, tiger's eye, turquoise.

Dreams – Amethyst, azurite.

Fertility – Aquamarine, aventurine, black coral, fluorite, jade, moonstone, pearl, red carnelian, rhodonite, rose quartz, smoky quartz, turquoise, unakite, zoisite.

Friendship – Chrysophrase, pink tourmaline, turquoise.

Grounding – Hematite, moonstone, obsidian, black tourmaline.

Happiness – Amethyst, chrysophrase.

Healing – Agate, amber, amethyst, bloodstone, calcite, carnelian, chrysophrase, quartz, garnet, hematite, hag stones, jasper, jet, lapis lazuli, sodalite, sugilite, turquoise.

House and home – Amethyst, aquamarine, aventurine, blue tourmaline, calcite, carnelian, chrysophrase, citrine, clear quartz, lepidolite, obsidian, rhodocrosite, rose quartz, turquoise.

Love – Amber, beryl, calcite, chrysocolla, emerald, jade, lapis lazuli, lepidolite, moonstone, pearl, sapphire, topaz, pink tourmaline, turquoise.

Luck – Apache tear, aventurine, chalcedony, chrysophrase, opal, pearl, tiger's eye, turquoise.

Meditation – Geodes, sapphire, sodalite.

Money & prosperity – Aventurine, bloodstone, calcite, emerald, jade, opal, pearl, peridot, sapphire, tiger's eye, topaz, green tourmaline.

Peace – Amethyst, aquamarine, aventurine, calcite, carnelian, lepidolite, obsidian, rhodocrosite, blue tourmaline.

Protection – Agate, amber, apache tear, calcite, carnelian,

chalcedony, chrysophrase, citrine, quartz, fossils, garnet, hag stones, jade, jasper, jet, lapis lazuli, lepidolite, malachite, moonstone, obsidian, petrified wood, serpentine, sunstone, tiger's eye, black tourmaline.

Psychic powers – Amethyst, azurite, beryl, citrine, quartz, hag stones, lapis lazuli.

Releasing and banishing – Amethyst, aquamarine, blue kyanite, chrysocolla, citrine, howlite, moonstone, obsidian, petrified wood, pyrite, rose quartz, rutilated quartz, selenite, smoky quartz, sugilite.

Sleep – Moonstone, peridot, blue tourmaline.

Success – Amazonite, chrysophrase.

Wisdom – Chrysocolla, coral, jade, sodalite, sugilite.

Colours

I love working with colour magic especially when working candle spells. Tie the colour of your candle, your medicine pouch or altar cloth into the intent of your spell to add an extra zing. Go with your intuition and what colours work for you. If you can't decide on a colour or you want to keep costs down go with simple white.

These are the colour associations I work with (taken from my book *Grimoire of a Kitchen Witch*):

Black – Protection, ward negativity, remove hexes, spirit contact, truth, remove discord or confusion and binding for spell work.

Dark blue – The Goddess, water elemental, truth, dreams, protection, change, meditation, healing.

Light blue – Psychic awareness, intuition, opportunity, understanding, safe journey, patience, tranquillity, ward depression, healing and health.

Brown – Endurance, houses and homes, uncertainties, influence friendships.

Green – Earth elemental, nature magic, luck, fertility, healing, balance, courage, work, prosperity, changing directions or attitudes.

Indigo – Meditation, spirit communication, karma workings, neutralize baneful magic, word slander.

Lilac – Spiritual development, psychic growth, divination, Otherworld.

Orange – The God, strength, healing, attracting things, vitality, adaptability, luck, encouragement, clearing the mind, justice, career goals, legal matters, selling, action, ambition, general success.

Pink – Honour, morality, friendships, emotional love, social ability, good will, caring, healing emotions, peace, affection, nurturing, romance and partnerships.

Purple – Power, spirit, spiritual development, intuition, ambition, healing, wisdom, progress, business, spirit communication, protection, occultism, self-assurance.

Red – Fire elemental, strength, power, energy, health, vigour, enthusiasm, courage, passion, sexuality, vibrancy, survival, driving force.

White – Purity, protection, truth, meditation, peace, sincerity, justice and to ward doubt and fear.

Yellow – Air elemental, divination, clairvoyance, mental alertness, intellect, memory, prosperity, learning, changes, harmony, creativity, self-promotion.

Ink and paper

Colour magic can be extended to the colour of ink you use to write your spells and petitions with and the colour of paper you write it on. Add in a drop or two of your essential oil blend to the ink or dab it on the paper for more layers of magic.

Astrological

If astrology is your thing, then you can tie your spell working in with the position of the planets. Working a spell that corresponds to the energy of a specific planet when it is dancing in the forefront of our skies will add extra kick to your magic. You can find all sorts of websites on the net that give you the current and future planetary positions.

Mars

Work spells for: Confidence, self-assertion, aggression, sexuality, energy, strength, ambition, impulsiveness, sports, competition, physical activity, passion, adventure, healing for trauma and fever, discipline, will power, stamina, attacks, defence, warriors, battles and breaking binding and love spells.

Venus

Work spells for: Love, beauty, passion, harmony, balance, feelings, sympathy, pleasure, sensuality, comfort, romance, marriage, business partnerships, sex, the arts, social life, grace, charm, healing, garden magic, immortality, relationships and female health.

Mercury

Work spells for: Communication, information and networking, travel, trade, merchants and commerce.

Moon

Work spells for: Emotions, unconscious habits, rhythms, memories, moods, adapting, reactions, maternal instincts, nurturing, the home, security, the past, healing, growing, cycles, domestic issues, marriage, female issues, female fertility, children, balance and secrets.

Sun

Work spells for: Ego, life force, creativity, male fertility, parenthood, sports, holidays, recreation, social events, healing, protection, prosperity and wealth.

Pluto

Work spells for: Renewal, rebirth, clarity, research, uncovering information.

Jupiter

Work spells for: Religion, faith, legal matters, politics, authority, influence, power, fatherhood, purification and healing.

Saturn

Work spells for: Leadership, law, order, rules, boundaries, death, taxes, fate, adversity and survival.

Uranus

Work spells for: Wisdom, individuality, new ideas, discoveries, inventions, groups and clubs, changes, freedom, healing for depression and breakdowns, revolution and originality.

Neptune

Work spells for: Dreams, visions, imagination, the arts, illusions, mysticism, spirituality, the divine, divination, water magic and healing.

Zodiac signs

And of course, if you like astrology you will probably have an interest in the zodiac too. Working a spell that corresponds with the current zodiac sign will also throw more power in.

Aries

Work spells for: Courage, authority, leadership, power, the forces, will power, new beginnings, challenges and protection.

Taurus

Work spells for: Stability, health, assistance, marriage, family, material gain, careers, financial stability and healing.

Gemini

Work spells for: Communication, neighbours, travel, siblings, transport, knowledge, education, activity, imagination, divination, wishing spells, luck and success.

Cancer

Work spells for: Family, home, domestic situations, gratitude, blessings spells, comfort, abundance, prosperity, love, luck and cleansing.

Leo

Work spells for: Courage, the arts, public speaking, fertility, childbirth, healing, influence, success, goals, removing obstacles, creativity and confidence.

Virgo

Work spells for: Employment, foundations, planning, organisation, financial planning, communication, clarity, precision, research, paperwork, details and healing.

Libra

Work spells for: Creativity, expression, partnerships, legal matters, balance, new love, new projects, truth and justice.

Scorpio

Work spells for: Luck, psychic abilities, mental issues, inner work, secrets, cleansing, reincarnation, past lives, karma, enemies, spirituality and magic of all kinds really.

Sagittarius

Work spells for: Travel, legal matters, publishing, healing, growth, spiritual relationships, creativity, co-operation, sharing, business success, transformation, inspiration, new beginnings, expanding, removing obstacles, releasing and meditation.

Capricorn

Work spells for: New business, new projects, planning, growth, organisation, foundations, ambitions, strength, health, banishing debt, clearing out, removing obstacles, rules, boundaries and elimination of pain.

Aquarius

Work spells for: Inspiration, innovation, clarity, social events, friendships, moving forward and solving issues.

Pisces

Work spells for: Dreams, astral travel, past lives, reincarnation, karma, psychic abilities, creativity, the arts and re-connecting with your spiritual path.

Deity

Inviting deity to add energy and assistance to your spell work is a bit like praying to a specific god. Choose one that aligns with the intent of your spell, you don't want to involve a warrior god when you are working with a love spell (let's not even go there). Be polite, mind your manners and treat deity with respect. Ask for their help rather than demanding it and don't forget to thank them afterwards, and an offering wouldn't go amiss, either.

Animal energy

Working with the energy of spirit animal guides in magic is powerful and rewarding. Think about the intent for your spell and then an animal that you believe represents it, or could lend their own characteristics to the working. All you need do then is invite that spirit animal guide to throw some of their energy into the spell pot. Go with your intuition on this and match your intent to the character and mannerisms of the animal. Here is a small list to give you an idea.

Call upon:

Bat – to avoid obstacles.

Bear – for wisdom and maternal instincts.

Butterfly – for transformation.

Cat – for independence.

Dolphin – for healing.

Frog – for new beginnings.

Horse – for letting out your wild side.

Magpie – for communication.

Peacock – for confidence.

Phoenix – to rise from the flames.

Rat – to overcome hatred.

Robin – for luck.

Selkie – to heal broken love.

Squirrel – for money matters.

Swan – for beauty and grace.

Unicorn – for purity.

Whale – for balance and relaxation.

Wolf – for overcoming your enemies and/or protection.

Symbols

All sorts of symbols can be used in spell work to add that extra power to your magic. Probably the most recognised within paganism is the pentagram, the five-sided star or the pentacle with the circle around the edge. Runes and ogham symbols are also good to use in spells but you can work with any symbol that you feel drawn to. Even something simple like a heart shape to correspond with the intent of love.

Symbols can be carved into candles, drawn onto paper for petitions or with chalk or created with magic powder, sand or salt.

Create symbols that represent your intent such as the heart for love or a dollar or pound sign for money. But you can also draw symbols to represent the deity you may want to call in; Hecate for instance has a wheel symbol.

In Voudou each loa (divine spirit) has its own unique veve, a symbol that is drawn to represent the loa. They are drawn and then used to place food or offerings on and often drawn on the floor during ritual using brick dust, flour or cornmeal.

You could look up to see if your deity has a specific symbol or you could create one. A simple image of a hammer would work for Thor or a spiral for any of the crone goddesses. The moon symbols also work well for the maiden, mother and crone or the phases of the moon.

The elements can be represented by their triangle symbols:

Air – an upright triangle with a line running horizontally across it.

Fire – an upright triangle.

Water – a triangle pointing downwards.

Earth – a triangle pointing downwards with a line running horizontally across it.

You don't have to be particularly artistic and it doesn't need to be detailed, just keep it simple.

Kitchen Witch Magic Cauldron of Spells & Charms

In this section I have listed various spell workings. Sometimes I have made suggestions for herbs, essential oils or colours of candle to use, these are my own preferences but I wholeheartedly encourage you to trust your own intuition. Be guided to use whatever herbs, oils or colours speak to you, or what you have to hand. Spell working should not cost a fortune and a good Kitchen Witch will use whatever they have in the cupboard. By tweaking the spells here and adding your own choices you are making the spell more personal. What works for one person may not work for another, it is your choice. Trust in yourself.

Curses, Hexing and Binding

I have already cast my waffle about cursing and hexing earlier in the book so the call is yours to make ... here I have shared some ideas for curses but also spells to remove them ... just in case you get hit.

If, when working a curse or hex some of the spell ingredients accidentally fall upon you then I would advise stopping the spell and focusing on cleaning and cleansing yourself. You don't want to go around hexing yourself!

Crystals to work with for curse and hex spells: Agate, alexandrite, amethyst, angelite, diamond, emerald, flint, shark teeth, garnet, hematite, kunzite, kyanite, obsidian, onyx, opal, ruby.

Herbs to work with for hex breaking spells: Angelica, cinquefoil, comfrey, datura, elder, horseradish, lily, rue, snapdragon, thistle.

Herbs to send negative intent and energy back to its source: Agrimony, blackthorn, elder, ginger, mullein, nettle, rue, thistle, willow.

Herbs for cursing: Cypress, dragon's blood, rowan, wormwood, yarrow.

Day of the week for curse and hex spells: Wednesday.

Planets for curse and hex spells: Mars, Jupiter, Saturn.

Zodiac signs for curse and hex spells: Scorpio, Sagittarius, Pisces.

Moon phases for curse and hex spells: Waning moon, dark moon.

Colours for curse and hex spells: Black, purple, red.

Cursing Stones

Charging a stone with malevolence is an ancient Celtic method of delivering a curse.

This is done when you are feeling full of negative emotions such as rage, anger and hatred; you direct all those emotions into the stone. It can then be stored and used later by taking up the stone in your hands, turning it widdershins (anti-clockwise) and directing those emotions to where you want them to go.

(This is also a useful way of venting all that anger and frustration by sending it into the stone; you could then drop it into the sea or a river so that those negative emotions wash away.)

Agate curse

Inscribing your curse onto an agate will 'set your curse in stone'.

Bad ass blueberries

Yep, the seemingly innocent blueberry can be used in a hex. Crush up a handful of blueberries until you get a nice dark pulpy mess and drop it onto the doorstep of your target.

Bottle hex

You will need:

A bottle or jar with a lid

A photograph of your target or their name on a slip of paper

Hexing herbs (whatever you feel drawn to use)

Vinegar (from an empty pickled onion or beetroot jar works well)

Black ink

Place the photograph or name slip in the bottle then fill it up with the other ingredients, quantities as you see fit. Seal the bottle and bury it upside down.

A misfortune hex:

You will need:

A slip of paper

A pen with black ink
A black candle
A cauldron or fireproof dish
Lighter/matches

Write the name of your enemy on a piece of paper in black ink, write the name nine times. Light a black candle and say out loud:

*I curse and hex thee *insert name of enemy**
Let it be done

Then light the piece of paper in the candle flame, drop it into a fire proof container to burn out.

To break a hex

If you feel that you have been hexed, this should break the link and return it to them:

You will need:
A sprig of rosemary
A piece of paper
A red pen
Scissors
A piece of red cloth
Paprika or chilli pepper
Red cotton

Keep the rosemary on your person whilst you work this hex. Write the name of the person who has hexed you on a piece of paper, if you don't know who did it just write "enemy mine". With the red pen, draw a doll shape around the name and cut it out. Lay the paper doll face down on the red cloth and sprinkle it with paprika or chilli pepper. Tie the cotton around the middle of the doll then wrap it in the red cloth, hold it in your hands and say:

>*Enemy of mine your power is gone*
>*The hex is broken, the spell undone*
>*Enemy mine go away*
>*So shall it be from this day*
>*This spell will last until your apology sets you free by me*
>*This is my will, so mote it be*

Perform this chant for seven nights in a row, then unwrap the doll, tear it into nine pieces and burn it. Scatter the ashes somewhere away from your home and dispose of the red cloth.

A cord binding spell

You will need:

A piece of cord or string

Cast a circle, using cord or string, think of what you want to bind. Say in a strong voice:

>*The first knot binds in my intent*
>*The second knot binds ill wishes*
>*The third knot binds it all together*
>*These knots shall hold the spell*
>*Until these knots are all undone*

As you speak a line, tie one knot. The first knot should be at one end, the second in the middle. The final knot should be placed at the other end. As you tie the knots, visualise what you are binding being stopped from doing harm. Once the knots are tied, see the spell being continued until the knots are untied.

To unbind a binding spell

Some binding spells can cause physical effects. You might feel that you have invisible strands of hair or thin strings wrapped around you. You won't be able see them but you will feel them and nothing you do can make that sensation stop. Here is a way to dispel a binding.

You will need:

A small piece of your own hair
3 candles – one red, one white and one green
Cauldron or fire proof bowl
Charcoal
Loose incense blend for releasing
Sterile pin

Light the three candles. In your cauldron light the charcoal and add the incense blend. Take the sterile pin and prick your right index finger, squeezing three drops of blood on top of the incense. Next drop in your piece of hair and say a chant:

My blood drops times three
This binding shall no longer be
The hair that burns is part of me
Allow me now to be bind free

Let the incense burn out and scatter the ashes outside.

To remove a curse

The occurrences of people being cursed are rarer than you might think. Contrary to what Hollywood would have you believe … However if you think it has happened to you then this spell might help.

You will need:

A bottle or jar
Some string

Wrap the string around the bottle/jar neck and tie a knot saying:

Any curses placed on me
I now bury in the earth deeply
The string I knot, once and twice
To turn the luck and make it nice

Now bury the bottle in your garden or if you don't have one bury it in a bucket or pot of soil. Leave it buried for as long as you think it needs, but I would suggest three, six or nine days as those numbers often work well.

Unearth the bottle; hold it in your hands and say:

The curse was buried deep
The hold over me can take a leap

Now smash the bottle and dispose of the broken glass.

Love Spells

Check the section earlier in the book for my views on love spells ... the choice, as always is yours to make.

Love correspondences

Crystals to work with for love spells: Amber, beryl, calcite, chrysocolla, emerald, jade, lapis lazuli, lepidolite, moonstone, pearl, sapphire, topaz, pink tourmaline, turquoise.

Herbs to work with for love spells: Agrimony, ash, aster, basil, benzoin, betony, birch, bleeding heart, caraway, cardamom, catnip, chamomile, chestnut, chickweed, cinnamon, cinquefoil, cleavers, clove, clover, coltsfoot, columbine (aquilegia), copal, coriander, cornflower (batchelor's buttons), crocus, cumin, cyclamen, daffodil, daisy, dandelion, dill, dittany of Crete, dock, dragon's blood, dulse, elm, fern, frankincense, geranium, ginger, hawthorn, hazel, heather, horehound, hyacinth, iris, ivy, jasmine, juniper, lady's mantle, lavender, lemon balm, lilac, lobelia, lovage, mallow, mandrake, marjoram, meadowsweet, mistletoe, myrtle, orchid, pansy, passion flower, periwinkle, poppy, primrose, rose, rosemary, rowan, Saint John's wort, sandalwood (red) , sea holly, sorrel, thyme, tulip, valerian, vervain, violet, willow, yarrow.

Day of the week for love spells: Friday.
Planet for love spells: Venus.
Zodiac signs for love spells: Libra, Cancer.
Moon phases for love spells: Full moon, Dark moon.
Colours for love spells: Red, pink.

Flower blossom name love spell

This is a variation on the old 'throw a piece of apple peel over your shoulder and see what letter it forms' spell to find out the first letter of the name of your new love.

You will need:

A handful of small flower heads or large flower petals (violet flower heads or rose petals work well).

Take the flowers in your hand and standing outside facing west think about love and being part of a happy couple. Throw the flowers in the air. Where the flowers land should (hopefully) show you a letter of the alphabet.

Rose petal new love spell

Cast this spell on a new moon to bring new love into your life.

You will need:

A rose petal in a colour you associate with love
A piece of paper
A new, unused pen
A candle in a colour you associate with love
A new, unused envelope

Take the paper and the pen and sit somewhere quiet and comfortable, on the day of a new moon. Write your request on the paper. It can be a chant or rhyme but also just heartfelt words will work. Something like:

On this new moon night
As my candle shines bright
Bring my new love to me
So mote it be!

When night falls set your candle on a window sill and light it. Sit or stand in front of the candle and read out your written words. Then hold the petal in front of the candle until you can see the flame through it. Place the petal and the written spell in the envelope. Seal it with a drop of the candle wax. Put the envelope on your altar or in a safe place. This should work within the monthly cycle of the moon.

Notice me spell

This works if you fancy someone and they haven't noticed you yet. There is no guarantee that once they do notice you there will be a connection, but if you don't try you won't know; although, you might want to take a moment to think about why they haven't noticed you yet. Maybe they really are not right for you or perhaps they are in a happy solid relationship already. The challenge for this spell will be obtaining the main ingredient ...

You will need:

A few strands of the other person's hair.
Incense of your choice (it might be your favourite scent or one that reminds you of them)

Light the incense and sit quietly allowing the aroma to fill your space. As it does repeat a chant starting with the other person's name, something like:

..*.insert name*... see me know
Come notice me
Turn your head
And make a vow

Say the chant a number of times until you feel ready, then hold the hair close to the incense so that it singes the ends. Visualise a veil being lifted from their eyes and a happy ending for you both as a couple. Let the incense burn out. Obviously, you will have to make sure you find yourself in the same location as the other person on occasion for them to be able to physically notice you.

Attention seeds spell

If collecting hair from the person of your desire is too much of a challenge (and I can totally understand that it would be) then you could try this spell to help attract their attention. Work it on a new moon for the best result.

You will need:

A packet of seeds
A flower pot
Compost
A small coin

Hold your coin up to the new moon and get an image of the person you desire in your mind. Then take the coin and bury it at the bottom of the pot. Fill with compost and sprinkle the seeds on top forming the shape of the first letter of your desired person's name. If the pot is big enough shape the first letter of their surname too. It helps to be more specific …

Tend to your seeds; watering them and giving them plenty of warmth and light. Once the seeds begin to shoot, your new love should begin to take root. If the seeds don't germinate perhaps you were looking at the wrong target? (Or you're a terrible gardener … just a thought).

Bay leaf light my fire spell

If the passion in your relationship needs a bit of a boost this is a good spell for you.

You will need:

Sprigs of bay leaves
Fire

This works with a bonfire, open fire, fire pit, chimenea or even a BBQ.

Sit and watch the embers in the fire and see your partner in your mind's eye. As you focus on them throw some bay leaves onto the fire saying:

Bay leaves, as I throw you in the fire
Bring love and passion to my desire

Once the leaves have burnt, repeat the process for a total of three times.

Roses in the stream love spell

For those looking for love to come their way but with no one specific in mind, this is for you.
You will need:

Rose petals
Flowing water

Obviously, this works best by a river or a stream but at a push you could use the tap in your kitchen or bathroom but it will probably block up the plug hole …

Sit by the running water and think about the qualities you would like in a partner. It might be; kindness, generosity, manners – you get the gist. Say each quality out loud and drop a rose petal into the water for each one, as you visualise the qualities. Once you are done, drop the last petal into the water saying a closing statement such as:

As the petals wash down the stream
Bring to me with love
The one about whom I dream

Bind us together love spell

This is a nice spell to work to affirm your feelings as a couple.

Make sure your partner understands what they are doing and what they are committing to. I have had a few people come to me who think they may have been bound to another before the relationship ended and subsequently cannot maintain a long term relationship with anyone else because they were still bound to the previous partner.

You will need:

A twig of herbs that can be split in two (bay works well, so does rosemary)
A hair from your head
A hair from your partner's head
A ribbon or twine (it is a nice touch to use red or pink)

Sit facing your partner and split the herb down the centre. You keep one half and give the other to your partner. Hold the herbs in front of you and each person should kiss the leaves. Then you give your herbs to your partner who will bind them with their hair. As they bind they should make a statement, along the lines of:

Let our love be bound together
So our lives are entwined forever

Then you tie your hair around the herbs saying the same chant. Finish by binding the herbs and hair with ribbon or twine and hang it somewhere so that you will both see it regularly.

Bring together sugar spell
To bring you together with someone who is lacking commitment. This does tread on the edge of 'free will' so think about it carefully; it is your call … However, it can also be used as a nice commitment spell for a couple to work together.

You will need:

A tablespoon of granulated brown sugar
A teaspoon of alcohol such as brandy
A cauldron or fireproof bowl
Lighter

Put the sugar in the cauldron and pour some alcohol into the teaspoon. Set light to the alcohol and slowly pour it onto the sugar. It should stay alight. If it doesn't then the timing is not right for this spell, try again later. If the flame stays alight say your spell:

As you burn a sweet flame
Bring to me this person I name
Entwine us together as one heart
As it is so, may we never part
Repeat the chant until the flame goes out.

Unwanted advances spell

If you are being pursued by someone whose advances are not welcome this may help get rid of them, not in a final 'in a coffin' kinda way but out of your life. Although I would suggest your first course of action is to tell them firmly that you are not interested (nicely of course).

You will need:

Herb leaves (something that banishes or removes such as rosemary, mint or mugwort)
A fire

Once your fire is burning nicely throw a handful of the herbs onto the flames. Call out the name of the person very loudly and with feeling. Then say:

Leave me now

Go, depart
I care not how
You are not in my heart
With no return

Visualise the flames and smoke removing that person from your life.

Love bread spell

This works to draw someone to you but also to help love grow with the proving of the yeast and the raising of the dough.

You will need:

A bread recipe and the ingredients

Make the bread according to the recipe and once you have worked the final kneading and shaping carve the initials of your intended into the top of the dough. As the bread bakes in the oven visualise you both being happy together. An added boost to this spell is if you can share the bread with that person too.

Adding passion spell

You will need:

A ring you wear and one your partner wears (wedding rings are perfect for this)
Essential oil you associate with passion, so maybe cinnamon or ginger, something fiery!

Charge the oil with your intent. Rub a little of the oil around the inside of each ring and put the rings back on the respective fingers.

Et voila! Va va voom installed ...

Together rings

This is for a couple who are going through a bad patch or even friends who have argued.

You will need:

A ring from each person
A piece of thread – colour of your choice

Hold one ring in each hand and visualise love, happiness and belonging flowing between them. Make sure the energy flows both ways.

Then tie the rings together with the thread and put them on your altar or on your bedside table.

Draw love bottle

If you want to attract a specific person you could put a photograph of them in the bottle. If you don't have anyone specific in mind you could write qualities that you admire on slips of paper to pop in the bottle instead. Something like 'kind', 'patient', 'sense of humour'.

You will need to add either some dirt from your garden, a cobweb or some dust from your house (obviously none of us ever have dust or cobwebs in our houses … ahem).

A strand of your hair can go in too, then some love and passion herbs and spices. Check your kitchen cupboard and be guided by your intuition but spicy, hot things such as cinnamon and love herbs like lemon balm work well.

Once you have all your ingredients in the bottle, breathe into it three times, visualising yourself in a strong and happy relationship.

Then put a stopper in and put it under the bed or in a drawer of your bedside table.

And the end ...

If a romance has finished and you are done with it (be very certain you are), but the other person is 'hanging on' work this bottle spell.

You will need:

A bottle or jar
A photograph of both of you or a memento that symbolises the relationship
A spoonful of vinegar

Put the photograph or memento in the bottle and pour in the vinegar. Seal and bury away from your home.

Prosperity, Wealth and Money Spells

I don't think there are many of us that couldn't use an extra few folding notes in our wallets. Help yourself by looking for mundane actions (yep, you know that 'hard work' thing) to help assist your finances too, don't let magic take all the strain.

Crystals to work with for prosperity, wealth and money spells: Aventurine, bloodstone, calcite, emerald, jade, opal, pearl, peridot, sapphire, tiger's eye, topaz, green tourmaline.

Herbs to work with for prosperity, wealth and money spells: Ash, basil, benzoin, bergamot (orange), bladder wrack, calamus, camellia, cedar, chamomile, clove, clover, comfrey, coriander, dill, dock, fenugreek, flax, ginger, goldenrod, gorse, hazel, honesty, honeysuckle, jasmine, mandrake, mint, myrtle, nettle, nutmeg, oak, patchouli, periwinkle, poppy, scullcap, tulip, vervain, woodruff.

Days of the week for prosperity, wealth and money love spells: Wednesday, Thursday, Sunday.

Planet for prosperity, wealth and money love spells: Sun.

Zodiac signs for prosperity, wealth and money spells: Taurus, Cancer.

Moon phases for prosperity, wealth and money spells: New moon, full moon.

Colours for prosperity, wealth and money spells: Green, gold, yellow.

Bake it

You can add prosperity magic to your baking. If you are adding currents, sultanas, seeds, nuts or chocolate chips to the recipe as you add them in visualise them as gold coins.

With dough or pastry you can draw money symbols on the top; a dollar or pound sign or a rune such as fehu.

Money mirror charm

We could all do with a bit of extra cash now and then right? This spell makes a sweet little money charm to pop in your purse or bag.

You will need:

A tiny mirror about the size of a coin (like the ones used in crafting)

A small piece of green or gold material (or a colour you associate with money)

Hold the mirror in front of you and tell it what you desire, speak directly into the mirror with your wishes. Repeat your desire three times (or more if you feel the need to). Wrap the mirror in the piece of cloth. Say a chant:

With blessings of money, wealth and cash
May the universe provide me with what I need
Help me create a money stash

Pop the charm into your purse or wallet, it works best if it is next to money or where you keep your money.

Re-charge the charm when you have received three unexpected amounts of cash coming in.

Drawing money jar spell

This spell uses the magic of the number five which corresponds to risk taking and change.

You will need:

Five of each of four different coins (so that makes a total of twenty coins) it only needs to be small change denominations, so you might want to empty your pockets and check down the back of the sofa.

Then you need herbs and spices to add to your jar, I have given some examples below but go with what feels right for you or whatever you have in the cupboards, just make sure you add five of each:

5 cloves
5 cinnamon pieces
5 sesame seeds
5 nuts
5 grains of rice
5 teaspoons of oatmeal
5 dried corn kernels
5 dried mint leaves

And of course, you will need a clean jar or bottle to put it all in, make sure the neck is big enough to fit the coins through.

Charge each ingredient (including the coins) with the intent of drawing prosperity and wealth to you then add it to the jar.

Seal the container with a secure lid and shake the bottle five times, saying a chant such as:

Coins of silver and copper shine
Prosperity and money be mine
By the power of magic five
Bring this luck spell to life

Put the jar in a place where you leave your wallet or purse when you are at home.

Planting money spell
If you spend time in the garden and like to plant seeds, this spell will be easy for you.

You will need:

Seeds
Plant pot
Compost
A coin

Fill the pot with compost then push a coin right down into the soil. Gold colour coins work well with the energy of the sun and silver coins work with the energy of the moon. Copper aligns with Venus so go with what feels right for you. You only need one coin in a pot but you can plant up as many pots as you want to.

Once the coin is buried sprinkle the seeds on top. Say a chant such as:

As I plant the seed
Money comes to my need
As the seedlings grow to full health
May the gods provide me with wealth
Look after your pots of seeds.

Candle and coin spell

This spell draws money to you using a candle. I would recommend a small rolled beeswax candle for this. Don't use a large taper or church candle because you need it to burn almost right down and you don't want to be sat watching a candle for days on end …

You will need:

A small candle, colour of your choice but I like green or gold
A coin
Essential oil blend (optional) I like basil, cinnamon or mint

Melt the base of the candle just enough to be able to press a coin into it. If you are using an essential oil blend dress the candle with it whilst visualising money coming to you. If you aren't using oil just hold the candle and visualise your desired outcome. Light the candle and chant:

Light of candle
Strength of flame
Multiply my coin of realm
May money come to me
So mote it be

Burn the candle until it is just down to the coin, then snuff it out.

Money flow spell

Work this spell on a full moon for extra power.

You will only need the money you have in your purse or wallet, no matter how little that might be!

This spell needs to be worked outside to help the energy flow and not be restricted by the walls of your home.

Lay the coins and notes you have in front of you and one by one turn them over. Repeat this chant:

By the power of the full moon
Allow the flow of money to me soon
Let prosperity find its way
Money rain upon me from this day

Then you can put the money back into your purse.

Protection Spells

Protection can be drawn in through a variety of ways, find one that works for you but here are some ideas.

Crystals to work with for protection spells: Agate, amber, apache tea, calcite, carnelian, chalcedony, chrysophrase, citrine, quartz, fossils, garnet, hag stones, jade, jasper, jet, lapis lazuli, lepidolite, malachite, moonstone, obsidian, petrified wood, serpentine, sunstone, tiger's eye, black tourmaline.

Herbs to work with for protection spells: African violet, agrimony, aloe, alyssum, anemone, angelica, ash, aster, basil, bay, benzoin, betony, birch, black pepper, blackthorn, bladder wrack, bluebell, borage, bracken, broom, burdock, buttercup, calamus, caraway, cardamom, carnation, cedar, celandine, chickweed, chrysanthemum, cinnamon, cinquefoil, clove, clover, comfrey, copal, coriander, cornflower (batchelor's buttons), cramp bark, cumin, cyclamen, cypress, daffodil, daisy, datura, delphinium, dill, dittany of Crete, dogwood, dragon's blood, dulse, elder, fennel, fern, feverfew, flax, foxglove, garlic, geranium, ginger, gorse, gourd, grass, hawthorn, hazel, heather, heliotrope, holly, honeysuckle, horehound, hyssop, ivy, juniper, lavender, lilac, lily, lobelia, lovage, mallow, mandrake, marigold, marjoram, mint, mistletoe, mugwort, mullein, mustard, myrrh, myrtle, nettle, nutmeg, oak, parsley, patchouli, pennyroyal, peony, periwinkle, pine, plantain, primrose, rose, rosemary, rowan, rue, sage, Saint John's wort, self-heal, snapdragon, Solomon's seal, star anise, sunflower, sweetgrass, sweet pea, tansy, thistle, tobacco, tulip, turmeric, valerian, vervain, violet, willow, witch hazel, woodruff, wormwood, yarrow.

Days of the week for protection spells: Tuesday, Thursday, Saturday.

Planet for protection spells: Sun.

Zodiac sign for protection spells: Aries.

Moon phases for protection spells: Waning moon, dark moon.

Colours for protection spells: Black, dark blue, purple, white.

Protection charm

You will need:

A small crystal, shell or similar item to use as a charm

This works well with a small crystal but you can use whatever you are drawn to, maybe a shell or a feather but you need to be able to carry the item with you.

If you can sit outside then do so. Make yourself comfortable with the crystal in front of you. If you are able to place it in direct sun or moonlight then even better, but in front of a candle flame also works well. Sit quietly and gradually enter a meditative state.

Allow the positive energy from the crystal to enter your body on each breath you draw in and allow any negative energy to escape each time you breathe out.

Next expand the energy from the crystal so that it starts to surround you with a strong positive light. Let it envelope you completely (but not restrictively) in a flexible bubble forming a body shield around you. Enjoy the feeling of protection, move about, stretch your arms and legs and feel how the shield moves with you.

When you are ready, focus on your breathing once more and allow the energy bubble to dissipate back into the crystal. Carry the crystal with you as a tool to tap into any time you need to activate a personal protection shield.

Verbal bullying protection spell

This is ideal for children to carry with them (and adults too). Let the person who the spell is for choose the crystal themselves, as children are especially intuitive when choosing crystals.

You will need:

A piece of cloth, felt or small drawstring bag
Ribbon (if using cloth or felt)
A crystal to bring peace
Essential oil blend for peace (I like lavender, rose and sweet pea)
A candle for peace (white or pink are both good)
A bay leaf (for protection and strength)
A piece of cinnamon (for power, protection and changes)
Dried lavender or lavender oil (for peace, protection and strength)

Anoint the chosen crystal with the essential oil blend, then anoint the candle too.

Light the candle and focus on the flame, see the anger and emotions associated with bullying leave, burnt away by the flame.

Take the bay leaf, piece of cinnamon and the crystal and charge them with your intent then pop it into the bag or onto the cloth. Sprinkle on some of the dried lavender or a drop of lavender oil, charging with your intent again. Tie the cloth up with ribbon or pull the drawstrings on the pouch closed.

Hold the pouch in front of the candle flame and charge it once again with your intent, to form protection around the bearer and to deflect any bullying.

If the pouch loses some of its power you can re-charge it again in front of the candle flame.

White light protection

This is a form of the protection 'bubble' and can be used for yourself or projected onto another person. If it is for someone else use a photograph to represent them if you can. I have used white because it is a good colour to work with for creating a protection bubble but if you prefer to use another colour, go with it.

You will need:

Incense or oil burner and oil – use a scent you associate with protection such as bay, rosemary or dragon's blood
White candle

Sit quietly and light the incense/oil burner and enjoy the fragrance for a moment. Then light the candle. When you are ready, call upon the Divine, deity or spirits of your choice to lend their protection. Visualise the light from the candle growing stronger and bigger until it wraps itself completely around you (or the image of another person).

Say something like:

White light protect me and keep me safe
Blessed be

Return to sender bottle

If you are experiencing bullying or hateful gossip from someone this should put a stop to it.

You will need:

A bottle
Small pieces of broken mirror or broken glass
A couple of rusty nails
Your urine (yep, you heard me)

Add all the items to the bottle, charging each one as you add it.
The mirror or glass is to reflect back the malicious behaviour.
The rusty nails represent the hurt and the harm.

The urine is to represent that you are literally 'peeing on their parade' and request that they 'pee off' ...

Bury the bottle on the edge of your property, in the direction that faces their house if possible.

Travelling protection spell

This travel spell brings protection by using the energy of the east and the air.

You will need:

A pebble
Paint or marker pens
Incense to represent air (lavender, mint or pine are all good)

Light the incense and sit facing east if possible with your pebble in front of you. Visualise having a safe journey. Then draw or paint an equilateral triangle with a line drawn across just above the base line. This is the symbol for air. Or if you prefer, draw a cloud or some wavy lines, something that represents air to you.

Next hold the stone up facing east and ask for the blessing of air for safe travel. Then carry the pebble with you.

On a safe return, I like to pop the pebble in the garden, returning it to Mother Nature as a thank you.

Protection bag spell for a child

This will keep a child from harm; they might also like to help when you create it.

You will need:

Protection herbs and spices
A coin minted in the child's year of birth
An initial bead or charm with the child's name on
A baby tooth (if you have one)
A pouch

Charge all the items with protection and pop them in the pouch; keep in a safe place until the child is old enough to look after it.

Courage and Confidence Spells

Even the bravest most courageous people get a fit of the wobbles occasionally, work some magic to give you a roar of lion's courage and a peek at peacock's confidence.

Crystals to work with for courage and confidence spells: Agate, amethyst, bloodstone, carnelian, lapis lazuli, tiger's eye, turquoise.

Herbs to work with for courage and confidence spells: Angelica, benzoin, birch, black pepper, borage, carnation, catnip, columbine (aquilegia), daisy, fennel, myrrh, plantain, sweet pea, thyme, yarrow.

Day of the week for courage and confidence spells: Tuesday.

Planet for courage and confidence spells: Mars.

Zodiac signs for courage and confidence spells: Aries, Leo.

Moon phases for courage and confidence spells: New moon, waxing moon.

Colours for courage and confidence spells: Green, red.

Parchment jar confidence/courage spell

This is a useful spell to boost your confidence, self-esteem and courage and to bring new friends your way if you are shy.

You will need:

Pen
Paper
Jar with a lid
Salt (nothing fancy, just table salt will do)

Sit quietly and write your personality traits and characteristics down on a sheet of paper. List the good and the bad. Then list your likes and dislikes.

Next, fill the jar about one third full of salt. Roll the list up and pop it into the jar, wedging it into the salt. Seal the jar. Focus on the jar and the list inside, visualise yourself the way you would like to be.

When you are ready say out loud:

The list inside is all of me
Open up the world for those to see
Confidence, courage and self-esteem
All of these traits from me will beam
Pop the jar on your altar or beside your bed.

Spell for confidence

We could all do with a confidence boost every once in a while; whether it is for self-esteem, an interview, at school or before exams.

You will need:

A slip of paper
A pen (can be coloured ink to bring in colour magic)
A crystal – red or orange crystals work well for this
Lighter/matches
Cauldron or fireproof dish

Write your request on the paper, it might just be 'give me confidence' but you can be more specific if you prefer. Hold the crystal in your hand and ask that you be blessed with courage, self-esteem and confidence. Visualise these qualities within you.

Then light the slip of paper and drop it into the cauldron. Watch the paper burn and send out your request again to the universe.

Carry the crystal with you.

Courage spell

You will need:

A tealight or candle
Essential oil for courage – something hot or spicy such as
cinnamon or dragon's blood
Incense of your choice
Crushed black pepper

Light the incense and allow the scent to fill the room. Put a few
drops of essential oil and a sprinkling of black pepper carefully
in the top of the tealight. Or if you are using a candle, dress it
with the oil blend and roll it in the black pepper.

Visualise yourself standing tall and proud and full of all the
courage you need. Draw in the energy from the incense, the oil
and the pepper.

When you are ready, say something out loud such as:

Strength and courage come to me
Inner roar and fiery flames
Fill my soul for all to see

Blow out the candle and stand up tall.

Proud as a peacock confidence spell

There is nothing more confident than a peacock strutting his
funky stuff with his tail feathers fanned out.

Use the image of a peacock in your mind from which to
borrow confident energy. You could carry a picture of one in
your pocket or pop an image on your altar. Carrying a piece of
peacock ore with you will also remind you that you are packed
full of self-confidence and able to strut with the best of them.

Thor's courage

The humble stinging nettle is sacred to Thor and was said to embody courage and strength. Carry some nettle leaves with you to bring the courage of Thor.

Luck Spells

I am a great believer in the idea that we create our own luck, good fortune and happiness. We really do hold our own destiny in our hands. However, we can all do with a bit of a boost from Lady Luck occasionally.

Any item of jewellery can be charged with luck (or any intent come to that). Or you could charge a pebble, shell or crystal and keep it in your bag or purse. Cleanse the item with smoke or visualise a white light clearing it from all negative energy. Then hold it in your hand and visualise luck coming your way and send that energy into the item. You could also use a chant such as:

By the power of three times three
Fill this charm with luck for me
With the magic power of old
Keep the flow of luck bold

Crystals to work with for luck spells: Apache tear, aventurine, chalcedony, chrysophrase, opal, pearl, tiger's eye, turquoise.

Herbs to work with for luck spells: Agrimony, aloe, angelica, beech, broom, calamus, clover, daffodil, elm, hazel, heather, holly, horseradish, marigold, nutmeg, oak, peony, poppy, rose, star anise, sunflower.

Days of the week for luck spells: Wednesday.

Planet for luck spells: Sun.

Zodiac signs for luck spells: Scorpio, Cancer.

Moon phase for luck spells: New moon.

Colours for luck spells: Green, orange.

Turn your luck around mirror spell

We all have periods when we feel that our luck is not helping us, so this spell will turn your luck around.

You will need:

Two small mirrors both the same size
Glue
Cord or ribbon

Place both the mirrors under the full moon or at noon under the sun.

Chant:

Send all negative energy and bad luck away
When the mirror does a turn
Bring in the positive and good luck today
Abundance, good fortune and luck will return

Glue the mirrors together back to back sticking a piece of cord or ribbon between them so you can hang them up. Pop the mirror over your altar. When you need to change the tide of your luck turn the mirror around whilst saying the chant.

Lucky bread spell

You will need:

A slice of bread
A nail
A piece of ribbon (traditionally purple)

Bang a nail in above your front door, tie a piece of ribbon to it and then hang the slice of bread on the nail. Replace as soon as the bread begins to rot or break down. Burn the old slice of bread. Note: Toasted bread will take longer to decay.

Lucky seven stone spell

Pick seven small crystals (ones that you don't mind losing) and place them under a full moon for seven hours. Next hold the stones in your hand and visualise them being filled with a bright green light and becoming empowered with luck. Pop the stones into a small pouch and carry with you. They will bring you luck but if you need an instant boost of good fortune chuck one into a river, ocean or stream.

Simple luck candle spell

You will need:

A candle in a lucky colour (red is traditional for this spell)
Essential oil luck blend

Hold the candle in your hands and charge it with your intent. Carve a symbol or letter into the candle to represent luck (such as a clover shape). Dress the candle with your oil. Burn the candle.

Foot track luck spell

This magic involves your foot prints and drawing luck into your home.

You will need:

Soil from underneath your own footprint
An equal quantity of dried herbs for luck such as patchouli or lemon balm
Ground cinnamon

Gather the soil from your own footprint and mix it together with an equal quantity of dried herb, sprinkle with ground cinnamon and mix together. Starting at the pathway to your home, walk towards your entrance sprinkling the powder right up to your front door.

Lucky ring spell

You will need:

A golden ring

On the first sighting of the new moon turn a golden ring three times widdershins (counter clockwise) to bring luck.

Key magic

Keys hold their own special kind of magic and are said to attract positive energy to you whilst also deflecting negative energy – perfect! Keys can open doors of opportunity, success, new ventures and all kinds of possibilities. Find yourself an old metal key and charge it with your intent.

Salty luck spell

On the first Friday of each month, sprinkle salt onto the front doorstep of your house to bring good fortune and luck for the month ahead.

Break bad luck spell

Sometimes it can feel as if we are sitting inside a spell of bad luck, this will help turn the tables.

You will need:

A white candle
Olive oil
Ground pepper (red is traditional, black will be OK)

Charge your candle with the intent to break the bad luck surrounding you. Dress it with the olive oil and roll in ground pepper. Light the candle and place it SAFELY on the floor and jump over it. Bad luck streak broken and the spell is done.

Employment Spells

Spells can help you secure an interview or even a job but it is no good working a spell and then sitting at home waiting, you need to go out there and look …

Crystals to work with for employment spells: Apache tear, aventurine, bloodstone, chalcedony, calcite, chrysophrase, green tourmaline, malachite, opal, pearl, tiger's eye, turquoise.

Herbs to work with for employment spells: Beech, bergamot (orange), cinnamon, clover, cumin, ginger, holly, lemon balm, lily of the valley, rowan, sage, Solomon's seal.

Days of the week for employment spells: Tuesday, Wednesday, Sunday.

Planets for employment spells: Mars, Mercury.

Zodiac signs for employment spells: Aries, Taurus, Leo, Virgo, Capricorn.

Moon phases for employment spells: New moon, waxing moon.

Colours for employment spells: Brown, light blue, green, orange.

New job mirror spell

This spell is to help you attract the best employment to suit you. You will need:

A small mirror
A magnet (smaller than the mirror)
Your business card or type of job you require written on a slip of paper
Essential oil for success, cinnamon or lemon balm work well
Glue or a rubber band

Dab the magnet with the oil.

Glue the business card to the back of the mirror (or place it for securing later with the rubber band).

Place the magnet on top of the business card (if using glue, stick it in place).

Now dab the edges of the mirror with the oil and visualise yourself gaining the best job you possibly could, do this as you focus on your reflection in the mirror.

Chant:

With this mirror and magnet back
The best job for me I will attract

Say the chant several times over, as many times as you feel is right but seven is a good number to work with.

If not using glue you will need to put a rubber band around the magnet, card and mirror to keep them together. Pop it in your bag or pocket and take it with you when you go for interviews focusing on it for a few seconds before you enter.

New job candle spell

You will need:

Two candles to represent the job
One candle for prosperity
One candle to represent you
Essential oil in an oil burner or incense for prosperity (basil, mint or cinnamon are all good)
Talisman of your choice

Place one of the job candles in front of you with the prosperity candle to the right of it and the personal candle to the left. Put your essential oil burner or incense in front of the job candle. Lay the other job candle on its side in front of that. Put your talisman in front of your personal candle.

Light the personal candle and focus on the flame, ask it to bring you clarity and opportunity.

Light the prosperity candle and focus on the flame, ask it to bring you luck and good fortune.

Visualise yourself accepting a new position and then light the job candle. Ask it to bring you a new fulfilling and suitable job.

Allow the candles to burn out and leave all the items in place. For the next few days light the second job candle each night and allow it to burn for nine minutes, focusing on your perfect new job as you do. Repeat until the candle is burnt out.

Personal stone job spell

You will need:

A stone or crystal of your choice

Hold the stone to your forehead and visualise the new job you would like. See the interview being successful. See the job offer. See yourself accepting it. Focus all that energy and direct it into the stone.

Put the stone by your computer when you type your job applications. Tap the stone on the envelope of each one before you post them.

Take the stone with you to interviews.

Offering interview spell

You will need:

A small glass of juice, your choice of flavour, whatever feels right for you
A candle to represent the job
A jar to hold the candle
Seven pebbles

On the morning of your interview light the candle and put it in the jar. If possible do this outside. Put the candle down and make a circle of the pebbles around it. Take the glass of juice and raise it to the rising sun and ask for courage and success in your interview.

Take a sip of the juice and pour the rest on the ground as an offering. Leave the candle and stones in situ (blow out the candle before you leave) and head to your interview with the energy of the sun behind you.

Healing Spells

Please bear in mind: Never stop taking your medicine without consulting a doctor first. Spells cannot take the place of medicine, what they can do is add their own unique magical power to the healing process.

Also remember that the universe, the divine or whatever higher power you believe in always has the last word. Sometimes you must accept that the cycle of life needs to happen.

Whether you send healing to another person without their permission is up to you. However, my personal belief is that you should, whenever possible, ask first, not everyone will want your help or indeed your (or anyone else's) healing. If you want to do something but are unable to gain permission, I would suggest working the healing spell and ask that the energy be sent 'to the universe to do what it will' with it. Kinda like a 'get out clause'.

Crystals to work with for healing spells: Agate, amber, amethyst, bloodstone, calcite, carnelian, chrysophrase, quartz, garnet, hematite, hag stones, jasper, jet, lapis lazuli, sodalite, sugilite, turquoise.

Herbs to work with for healing spells: Anemone, angelica, ash, bay, blackthorn, bluebell, bracken, burdock, calamus, caraway, carnation, cinnamon, coltsfoot, comfrey, coriander, cowslip, cramp bark, dock, echinacea, elder, eucalyptus, fennel, feverfew, flax, garlic, hazel, horehound, hyssop, ivy, juniper, knotweed, lemon balm, lungwort, marjoram, mint, mistletoe, mugwort, myrrh, nettle, oak, pine, plantain, rose, rosemary, rowan, rue, Saint John's wort, sorrel, tansy, thistle, thyme, vervain, violet, willow.

Day of the week for healing spells: Thursday.

Planets for healing spells: Mars, Venus, Moon, Jupiter, Uranus, Neptune.

Zodiac signs for healing spells: Taurus, Leo, Virgo, Sagittarius, Capricorn.

Moon phase for healing spells: Waxing moon.

Colours for healing spells: Dark blue, light blue, green, orange, pink, purple, red.

Candle healing spell

You will need:

A candle – a colour you associate with healing, I like to use blue

A photograph or something to represent the person requiring healing

Put the image of the patient in front of the candle and set their image in your mind. Light the candle and as it burns visualise the flame removing the illness and pain. See the patient regaining good health. You can add a chant:

See the patient, see them strong
Remove the illness and the pain
But don't prolong
Good health and happiness regain

Allow the candle to burn out fully.

Burning illness candle spell

To literally burn away illness, you can work this candle/petition spell.

You will need:

A candle, a colour to represent healing
Essential oil healing blend (optional)
A pen and paper

A cauldron or fire-proof dish

Dress the candle in oil if you wish. Write the name of the patient on a slip of paper and next to the name write:

Illness and pain dispel
So mote it be

Light the candle and visualise the person regaining good health and strength. Focus on the flame then when you feel ready set fire to the paper petition from the candle flame. Drop it into the fire-proof dish. Allow the candle to burn out. Send the ashes from the petition away on the wind or water.

Healing stone

This spell could not be any simpler and works for banishing negative energy as well as healing. Stones and shells from the beach are natural healing amulets. They have all the elements in one handy pocket size pack. Earth, because they are either a pebble or a shell that sits on the sand and in the salt water. Air, because they have been open to the sea breezes, fire from the baking sun and water, well that one is obvious, from the sea!

You will need:

A pebble or shell

Find a quiet place to sit undisturbed. Hold the pebble or shell over the area that is the centre of your illness. If you aren't sure exactly where that spot is, be guided by your intuition to find the right place. Your forehead or one of your main chakra positions often works well. Then focus and visualise your pain, hurt, illness or negative energy flowing from your body and mind into the pebble or shell. Take as much time as you need.

When you are ready, hold the stone or shell out in front of

you and visualise the negative energy being locked and sealed inside.

Then you need to get rid of the pebble or shell by throwing it into the sea, a river or throwing it away from a high place such as a hill. Failing that you can bury it away from your property (or anyone else's) or even as a last resort, drop it into the trash bin.

Carved candle healing spell

You will need:

A candle in a colour you associate with healing
A photograph of the patient requiring healing
Essential oil blend for healing (something like fennel, rosemary or thyme work well for me)
Nail, knife or sharp object for carving

Create your healing oil blend and charge it with healing energy.

Carve the name or just the initials of the patient into the candle. Dress the candle with the essential oil blend visualising the healing energy as you do so. You could chant as you dress the candle, perhaps:

Healing oil and candle power
Work my magic in this hour

Light the candle and place it on top of the photograph. If you feel that one small candle will do the trick then allow it to burn out. However, if the healing requires added strength you could use a larger candle and burn it for a few minutes each day over a period of several days. This allows the healing energy to build up and releases on the last day when the candle burns out.

Healing with the elements

You can bring in the power of all five elements for healing.

You will need:

A candle to represent each element; earth, air, fire, water and spirit – colours of your choosing

A photograph of the patient (or their name on a slip of paper)

Charge each candle in turn with the properties of each element; you could also dress them with a corresponding oil blend if you wish.

Place the candles in a pentagram shape, one candle at each point on a safe surface. Place the photograph of the patient in the centre.

Light each candle in turn saying:

Element of earth
Bringing your power of stability, grounding and strength
To heal *insert name of patient*
Element of air
Bringing your power of change and cleansing
To heal *insert name of patient*
Element of fire
Bringing your power of purification, rebirth and renewal
To heal *insert name of patient*
Element of water
Bringing your power of healing and balancing of emotion
To heal *insert name of patient*
Element of spirit
Who brings all the elements together
For healing power
So mote it be

Allow the candles to burn out.

Healing plant spell

If you would like to give a gift to someone is unwell, perhaps to lift their mood and brighten their room, you can add a dash of healing magic to it too.

You will need:

A pot plant you think the patient will like
A small crystal or two
Pebbles (optional)
Small shells (optional)

Pick a small crystal or two that 'speak to you', ones that you know will bring healing to your friend and charge them with your intent. You can also add small pebbles for grounding and stability and shells to help lift their emotions.

Either pop the crystals, stones and shells just on top of the soil in the plant pot or bury them just underneath the surface.

Gift the plant with love and healing.

Healing pouch spell

Either for yourself or someone else, this spell creates a small pouch of healing herbs that can be worn on a cord around your neck, carried in your pocket or put under a pillow.

You will need:

An essential oil blend for healing, echinacea, juniper or eucalyptus are all good but go with your intuition
A small piece of cloth or felt and ribbon to tie it or a drawstring bag
Mixture of healing herbs, three or four works well, something like bay, coriander, rosemary and lemon balm

Charge the essential oil blend and each of the herbs with your healing intent. As you do so, state the patient's name out loud followed by a chant such as:

With this healing in sight
I welcome the return of good health and might

Lay the cloth or bag out in front of you and take a good pinch of each herb and add it to the bag, saying:

Healing herbs if you may
Bring health all the way

Then add a couple of drops of the essential oil to the herbs in the bag. Gather up the edges of the cloth and tie with the ribbon or pull the drawstrings of the pouch tight.

Soak up pain spell

This spell can help take away pain and suffering.
    You will need:

Salt (table salt is fine for this but you can use rock or sea salt)
Candle (black works well)
A cotton wool ball or small piece of bath sponge
Dish of water (rain or spring if possible)
Empty dish or cup

You will need a space where you can put the items you are working with on a flat surface and be able to sprinkle salt around them to create a circle; on a table or a tray outside perhaps.
    Sprinkle the salt in a deosil (clockwise) direction around the items to form a circle.
    Light the candle and invite a deity, angel or spirit you like to work with to join you and bring blessings to the spell.
    Next dip the cotton wool or sponge into the water and see it soak up the liquid – this represents the pain. When the cotton

wool or sponge is fully soaked, move to the empty dish or cup and squeeze out as much of the water as you can.

As the water drips out say:

As the water flows out
And the sponge becomes dry
Leave me with no doubt
The pain will be gone, no more to cry

Place the cotton wool or sponge on top of a radiator or on a window sill until it is fully dry, then bury it.

Repeat the spell as many times as you need to.

Fertility Spells

Fertility doesn't just mean the pitter patter of tiny feet it can also mean fertility of new ideas, new beginnings and projects. Fertility of the procreation kind does need a bit of help, casting a spell can aid the process but obviously there are other things you will need to do too …

- **Crystals to work with for fertility spells:** Aquamarine, aventurine, black coral, fluorite, jade, moonstone, pearl, red carnelian, rhodonite, rose quartz, smoky quartz, turquoise, unakite, zoisite.
- **Herbs to work with for fertility spells:** Birch, bracken, catnip, chickweed, cornflower (batchelor's buttons), cyclamen, daffodil, dock, fennel, geranium, hawthorn, hazel, horsetail, mistletoe, mustard, oak, parsley, pine, poppy, sunflower, walnut.
- **Days of the week for fertility spells:** Monday, Friday.
- **Planets for fertility spells:** Venus, Moon, Sun, Jupiter.
- **Zodiac signs for fertility spells:** Taurus, Cancer, Sagittarius.
- **Moon phases for fertility spells:** New moon, waxing moon, full moon.
- **Colours for fertility spells:** Green, orange, red.

Fertile basil

Basil is perfect for working fertility spells, but keeping it simple, you can just have a pot of basil on your window sill or outside your door to encourage fertility. To aid specifically with conception keep a bunch of fresh basil hung over your bed. And of course, you can also eat the stuff!

Everyone's a fruit and nutcase

An ancient Chinese fertility spell involved throwing dates and nuts (chestnuts specifically) onto the bed to aid with conception. This sounds rather uncomfortable and perhaps a little messy so I would suggest popping a little bag full of them under the bed instead.

Rabbit fertility spell

We all know what rabbits are well known for doing ... use that energy to bring about fertility.

You will need:

A picture or image of a rabbit
Incense for fertility
Candles (optional)

Pop the image of the rabbit on your altar and light some incense, you can also light a candle or two if you wish. Focus on the image of the rabbit and ask for the gift of fertility. Visualise the new beginnings of your project, venture or adventure and see it coming to fruition.

Repeat this exercise daily until the seed has been planted ...

Bloodstone fertility spell

You will need:

One or two pieces of bloodstone crystals

Lay the bloodstone on your womb to stimulate fertility. Lie quietly for at least half an hour with the bloodstone in place, preferably on a new or full moon.

Cowrie shells for fertility

Shells in general are full of fertile energy but cowrie shells in particular work very well. It is said that part of the magic is because the cowrie shell is shaped like a yoni ... Make a necklace or a belt from cowrie shells sending your intent into the string and shells as you create it.

Egg fertility spells

And what could be more symbolic of fertility and tiny babies but an egg?

Place a pair of eggs in a bowl and cover them with water, keep the bowl under your bed, replace weekly (otherwise they might start to get a bit smelly).

Charge a raw egg with your intent and then bury it.

Decorate eggs with fertility colours and symbols then place them in a bowl or hang from a branch to form a fertility tree.

Fertility medicine bags

Create a medicine bag or pouch to carry with you, filled with herbs which you associate with fertility.

Mugwort bag – fill a red pouch with mugwort.

Charm bag – fill a bag with dried peas, jasmine flowers, and silver fish charms.

Fertility mojo – fill a bag with acorns, mistletoe and shells; dress with a fertility essential oil.

Cake fertility spell

One of my favourite ideas ... in Jewish traditions magical cakes are prepared for brides and women wishing to become pregnant. A round cake is decorated with the woman's name, names of power and sacred texts (you could use a chant). The woman then has to eat the whole cake ... sounds like a win win situation to me.

Nut and seed charms

Nuts and seeds all carry the magical property of fertility, use them to create a charm to wear.

You will need:

Nuts and seeds such as acorns, sunflower, pumpkin and melon seeds
Thread, in a colour you associate with fertility
A sharp needle
Incense for fertility

Soak the nuts and seeds in warm water for about an hour. Then thread them using a sharp needle to create bracelets and necklaces. You might need to drill holes in the nuts such as the acorns.

Pass the charms over incense smoke to activate the power.

Banishing and Releasing Spells

By banishing and releasing I mean letting go of the negative habits and energy that we sometimes acquire. All that niggling emotional stuff that holds us back.

Crystals to work with for banishing and releasing spells: Amethyst, Aquamarine, blue kyanite, chrysocolla, citrine, howlite, moonstone, obsidian, petrified wood, pyrite, rose quartz, rutilated quartz, selenite, smoky quartz, sugilite.

Herbs to work with for banishing and releasing spells: Alexanders, angelica, basil, bergamot (orange), birch, black pepper, blackthorn, carnation, celandine, clove, clover, coriander, cumin, cypress, daffodil, elder, garlic, heliotrope, horehound, horseradish, juniper, lilac, lungwort, mint, nettle, peony, rosemary, self-heal, Solomon's seal, thistle, thyme, willow, yarrow.

Day of the week for banishing and releasing spells: Saturday.

Planets for banishing and releasing spells: Moon, Pluto.

Zodiac signs for banishing and releasing spells: Aquarius, Capricorn, Sagittarius, Scorpio, Leo.

Moon phase for banishing and releasing spells: Waning moon.

Colours for banishing and releasing spells: Black, green, indigo, white.

Banishing mirror spell

Use this mirror spell to banish financial problems (or anything else for that matter, use the basic framework and adjust the chant to your requirement).

You will need:

A small mirror

Essential oil – your choice but something that banishes, so dragon's blood or clove would work well

Work this spell on a waning moon if possible. Hold the mirror in front of you and visualise a bright white light filling the mirror working from the outer edge into the centre. Then pop a dab of essential oil on your finger and dab it in the centre of the mirror, drawing out from there in a spiral to the edge of the mirror.

You can chant at this point, something like:

Mirror, mirror reflect for me
As the moon begins to fade
As the night turns to day
Release the night, turn on the light
Dispel bad luck and negativity
Financial worries let me be free

Place the mirror where it won't get knocked over but if possible put it so it faces outwards, perhaps through a window.

Angry egg spell

This isn't a spell to make eggs angry, but to release the anger and frustration we sometimes find ourselves hanging onto. Release the Kraken! Seriously, you will feel much better afterwards. Better to let it all go than allow it to fester 'coz then things can get really messy.

You will need:

Candle for anger and frustration (black or a dark colour)
Candle for self-worth and self-esteem (pink or yellow perhaps)
Candle for inner peace and clarity (white or pale blue work well)

An egg

You can work this spell indoors but you will need access to outside, somewhere that won't matter being covered in raw egg. If you are limited for space then it can be worked indoors but use the sink to throw the egg into.

Light the black candle and hold the egg with your fingers wrapped around the pointier end (this is the strongest point on the shell). Focus on the black candle flame and visualise all your anger and frustration flowing from you into the egg. Take as much time as you need, then throw the egg with as much force as you can muster shouting:

Anger and frustration leave me now!

Stand for a moment and allow the emotions to fade, then take some slow, deep breaths. Next make a statement out loud:

I release the anger and the pain and see the end of the frustration reign.

Extinguish the black candle.

When you are feeling calmer, light the candle for self-worth and self-esteem and the candle for inner peace and clarity. Watch the flames burn together side by side and say:

May the anger now be gone
The frustration and fear at an end
Calm, peace and self-worth to mend
I trust the anger to never return
Allow the two candles to burn out.

Smudging

Perhaps not technically a spell but it involves ingredients, actions to clear negative energy and a chant, so it has the elements of a spell and works well to clear negative energy and cleanse your home, sacred space or your body.

You can buy readymade smudge sticks or you can easily make your own by tying together bundles of herbs such as sage, rosemary and lavender or whatever you have growing in your garden really, then allow them to dry out. Failing that you can use an incense stick, cone or loose incense on a charcoal disc very effectively. I also like to use a big feather to waft the smoke.

It is up to you whether you walk around a room widdershins (anti-clockwise) or deosil (clockwise). Go with your intuition, some rooms may feel different to others. Generally, widdershins removes negative energy and deosil brings positive energy in but trust your instinct for each area.

Light the smudge stick and once you have some nice smoke start walking around the room or area. I like to start at the back of the house on the lower floor and move gradually through the rooms from back to front and then the same upstairs. Waft the smoke around each room making sure it goes into the corners. Chanting as you go:

Negative energy dispel
Make this home all well
Positive pure light come in
Happiness and love to win

Crystal programming spells

You can use the power of crystals to help you overcome negative ideas about yourself or stop unhealthy habits. Try using a crystal that you programme. Pick a crystal of your choice, one that your intuition tells you is correct. Hold it in your hand and tell it what you require of it, so it might be "I hate smoking cigarettes" or "I don't have any desire for eating cake" (as if …).

Wear the crystal or keep it in your pocket. When you feel

the desire come over you, touch the crystal to help alleviate the feeling and aid you in keeping your will power strong.

Returning hurt

There are situations where others hurt us intentionally. It is often difficult to shift the inner pain you are left with and you may also feel inclined to send the hurt back to them ... it is your call, if you choose to do so then this spell may be of use.

You will need:

A bottle with a lid or cork
3 nails or pins
A spring of rosemary
A small amount of milk
A small amount of vinegar
Salt

Put the nails, milk, vinegar and rosemary into the bottle and put the lid on. It will look pretty gross ...

Shake the bottle saying:

Wrongdoings
Spite and hate
The nasty and the hurt of late
Inside this bottle be done

Then dissolve some salt in a little warm water and swish it around your sink to cleanse. Next open the bottle top and pour the mixture down the plug hole saying:

The feelings within this bottle go out
And if the universe will
Turn them about

Throw the bottle away.

Clear the black dog spell

I am not going to say this spell will banish depression (the black dog) because that is a big statement to make but it can certainly help.

You will need:

A candle to banish (black is traditional)
A glass jug or vase ¾ full of water
A handful of soil
A bowl ¾ full of water
Rose petals (for love, peace, protection, healing and rebirth)

Light the candle and place the jug/vase of water in front of it so that you can see the flame through the water. Focus on the candle and visualise your life before the darkness set in. See it as clearly as you can see the flame through the water.

Next take a handful of soil and drop it into the jug of water then swirl it around with your fingers. As the earth makes the water cloudy see it as your depression and dark moods.

Say:

Dark waters deep
Dark moods to weep
Dispel, disappear and be gone

Sprinkle the rose petals onto the bowl of clean water and rinse your hands in it.

You can watch the candle burn out or snuff it and come back. But you need to leave the candle and jug in place long enough for the water to settle and clear.

Once you can again clearly see the flame through the water, say your chant again. Next take the jug of earthy water outside and throw the water away from you shouting:

Depression and dark inner fears … be gone!

Cord spell to let go

This spell helps to release and let go of grief, anger or guilt or any of those other nasty negative ninny feelings that sometimes engulf us.

You will need:

A piece of cord, thread or string
A knife or scissors

Tie a knot in one end of the cord – this represents you in the here and now complete with your grief, guilt or anger.

Hold the knot in your left hand and say:

This is me in the here and now
Full of anger/grief/guilt/*insert bad feeling here and how*

Take the other end with the knot in your right hand and say:

This is me as I want to be
Guilt, pain and anger free

Put the cord down in front of you and cut the cord in half.

Now pick up the cord on the left and untie the know saying:

Grief, pan and anger released

Bury this piece of cord or burn it.

Pick up the other end and keep the knot intact, place it on your altar or in a safe place as a reminder. When you feel all the negative emotions have been released you can dispose of this piece.

Rain spell to wash away

If you want someone or something out of your life you can literally wash them away.

Either, write down their name or the word that describes what bad habit or negative quality you want to be rid of and let the rain wash it away.

Write the name on the pavement in chalk or on a stone in your garden. Or write on a piece of paper and leave it pinned outside. You could also draw the name/word in sand or soil in your garden. Then just let the rain do its thing and wash it all away ...

Silencing gossip

It seems to be human nature that people love to gossip and the more hurtful and juicy the gossip is, the more the gossip mongers like it. This spell can put a stop to it.

You will need:

A candle – a hot fiery colour such as red or orange
A pen
A piece of paper
3 cloves
1 thorn
Cauldron or fireproof dish
Lighter/matches

Light the candle and visualise the faces of those who are gossiping. Write their names on the paper. If you don't know their names just write "those who are gossiping". Place the 3 cloves in the centre of the paper and fold it up to make a little parcel.

Hold the parcel and say:

Gossip stop, now at an end
See the gossip turn and bend
Let those at fault see the error of their ways
Shine a light back upon their says

Pin the thorn into the parcel and then burn or bury it.

House and Home Spells

Bless this house …

Crystals to work with for house and home spells: Amethyst, aquamarine, aventurine, blue tourmaline, calcite, carnelian, chrysophrase, citrine, clear quartz, lepidolite, obsidian, rhodocrosite, rose quartz, turquoise.

Herbs to work with for house and home spells: Any of the happiness, peace and love herbs.

Day of the week for house and home spells: Tuesday, Saturday.

Planet for house and home spells: Moon.

Zodiac signs for house and home spells: Taurus, Cancer.

Moon phase for house and home spells: New moon.

Colours for house and home spells: Brown, black, green.

Home blessing

Before you start the blessing for your home it is advisable to clean your house. Sorry … I know housework is boring but it makes sense to clean your home from top to bottom first. Once you are done if you have a besom (broom) it also adds a bit of magic cleansing to sweep the house symbolically. Sweep from the back of the house to the front, sweeping all the negative energy out of the door.

You will need:

Salt in a small bowl
Essential oil – your favourite scent
A candle
A few grains of rice
A square of fabric

Carry the bowl of salt to the back of the house and work your way around each room from the back to the front, downstairs to up. Sprinkle a pinch of salt in each corner or every room, on each window sill and above all the doorways.

As you sprinkle the salt say:

I cleanse and purify this room to dispel any negative energy

Once each room has been sprinkled with salt, light the candle. Take the candle in one hand and your oil in the other hand. Go through each room again, place the candle in the centre of the room as you anoint all the doorways and window frames with the oil saying:

I call upon the divine/angels/deity to bless this home, may it be forever filled with love, laughter and happiness

When you are done sit quietly and watch the candle burn down. Once it is nearly finished snuff the candle. Anoint the candle stub with your essential oil, sprinkle some grains of rice on it and wrap it in the piece of fabric. Place the bundle under your front door mat or as close to your front door as you can, saying:

All who pass through this door
Bring happiness, blessings and more

A protection spell for your home

I work this spell most nights just before I go off to sleep. It really is simple, all it requires is visualisation.

Relax and clear your mind then visualise a bright light coming up from the earth at the boundary of your home, allow the light to move upwards forming a large protective bubble around your home and garden. See it grow until it encapsulates the entire building and land.

Told you it was simple!

Happy family spell

This spell uses wolf energy; wolves have a very strong family bond within their pack. Use this energy for your own pack of humans.

You will need:

A strand of hair from each person in the family – you don't have to pull it straight from their head – you can take it from the hairbrushes
An envelope
A pen
Picture or image of a wolf

Take the hairs and twist them together, pop them in the envelope and write on the front of it. The words should come from your heart but something along the lines of "family bonds".

Put the envelope underneath the image of the wolf and keep it on your altar or tacked to the family notice board.

Dragon's blood happy home spell

You will need:

Dragon's blood resin
Salt
Sugar
A matchbox or small box
Envelope

Crush the dragon's blood resin and mix it with equal quantities of salt and sugar. Put the powder inside a matchbox. Pop the matchbox into an envelope and seal it. You might like to decorate the envelope first with runes or symbols. Place the envelope somewhere safe and out of sight to keep your home a happy and peaceful place.

General Spells

Flowers for intent

If you have a family member or friend that you are visiting and planning on taking flowers too, add a bit of magic to them. You can charge the flowers with your intent whether that is for friendship, love, happiness or healing – whatever you choose.

Cut out or purchase a gift tag and write your message on it and attach it to the flowers. Charge the gift tag and your flowers with your intent, saying something along the lines of:

Beautiful bounty of nature with your fragrant smell
Bring healing wishes and make *insert name* well

Or

Beautiful flowers fresh and bright
Bring happiness to *insert name* and make their mood light
You get the idea ...

Ring magic for wishing

You will need:

A ring
A full moon

Stand outside and hold the ring up to your eye so that you can look through it and see the full moon in the centre. Make a wish.

Seven days, seven colours spell

This one requires seven different coloured candles and a few minutes of your time each day for seven days (the name of the spell was a bit of a giveaway wasn't it?). Preferably work it so that the seventh day falls on a full moon.

You will need:

Seven candles, you can use the colours of the rainbow/ chakras; red, orange, yellow, green, blue, indigo and violet or colours of your choice. Each one will represent a planet and their associated qualities

Monday – Moon – emotions
Tuesday – Mars – activity
Wednesday – Mercury – communication
Thursday – Jupiter – growth
Friday – Venus – love
Saturday – Saturn – structure
Sunday – Sun – energy
Place the candles in a row, safely in secure holders.

On Monday, light the moon candle and say:

Light and energy of the moon, I ask of thee
Bring for my emotions, stability

Allow the candle to burn out if possible or for at least ten minutes whilst you sit and visualise being in control of your emotions.

On Tuesday, light the Mars candle and say:

Light and energy of Mars, I ask of thee
A life full of enjoyable activity

Allow the candle to burn out if possible or for at least ten minutes whilst you sit and visualise going out and doing those things that you enjoy.

On Wednesday, light the Mercury candle and say:

Light and energy of Mercury, I ask of thee
Clear and concise communication ability

Allow the candle to burn out if possible or for at least ten minutes whilst you sit and visualise clarity and clear communication between you and others.

On Thursday, light the Jupiter candle and say:

Light and energy of Jupiter, I ask of thee
Prosperity, abundance and personal growth for me

Allow the candle to burn out if possible or for at least ten minutes whilst you sit and visualise being financially safe and happy in yourself.

On Friday, light the Venus candle and say:

Light and energy of Venus, I ask of thee
Comfort, friendship and love for my family and me

Allow the candle to burn out if possible or for at least ten minutes whilst you sit and visualise being surrounded by good friends and a happy family.

On Saturday, light the Saturn candle and say:

Light and energy of Saturn, I ask of thee
Bring order, balance and structure to my life for me

Allow the candle to burn out if possible or for at least ten minutes whilst you sit and visualise having balance, order and structure to your home and work life.

On Sunday, light the Sun candle and say:

Light and energy of Sun, I ask of thee
Bring passion and fiery energy to me

Allow the candle to burn out if possible or for at least ten minutes whilst you sit and visualise your life being full of energy and passion.

Once you have worked with each candle spend a few minutes in reflection and note down what changes you can make in your life to bring about these qualities.

Gratitude spell

We all need to thank deity, the divine, the universe, whatever or whoever at some point and this is simple.

Take yourself outside and look up to the sky. Hold your arms up and give thanks for all that you have. Then put your hands to the ground and give thanks again.

You might also want to do something for Mother Nature such as feeding the birds or watering the plants.

Bay wish spell

Bay leaves lend themselves to wishes and are often big enough to write at least one or two words on. If your wish needs to be conveyed with more than a couple of words use a piece of paper as well.

You will need:

A bay leaf
Slip of paper (optional)
A pen
Lighter/matches
Cauldron or fireproof dish

Write your wish on a bay leaf, set fire to it and drop it into the cauldron to burn. If you want to write out a more detailed wish do so on a piece of paper and then wrap the paper around a bay leaf. Set fire to it as before.

Larger leaves can also be used for this spell and if you prefer not to burn them you can leave the leaf outside to rot down; although this method may take longer for the magic to work.

Magic box

I have a lovely Green Man box that I use to put spells in. Usually it is a cheque that I write on each new moon for abundance and prosperity. I fold the cheque and put it in the box with various herbs and whatever else I am drawn to use. The cheque sits in my 'spell box' until the next new moon when I take it out, burn it and replace it with a new cheque.

But this works with any spell working that you want to 'keep going' and to be kept hidden.

I also like to place petitions on my altar under goddess statues or rolled up and balanced in the lap of my Ganesha statue. Popping business cards for success or a job CV for luck under statues on your altar also works well too.

Overcoming obstacles

This one could not be simpler and only requires your visualisation skills. Sit quietly in a place where you won't be disturbed. Bring to mind the image of a horse and fences for it to jump over. See yourself riding the horse and jump over the fence. Keep riding around the course and jumping over obstacles. Each fence is the obstacle which is blocking your life path, jump over them to overcome it. Repeat the exercise daily until the obstacle has been removed.

Disposing of spells

A question I get asked a lot is 'what do I do with the left-over bits and bobs from a spell?' Well the answer is up to you for the most part, trust your intuition. Some spells will be specific and require you to let a candle burn out fully so you hopefully won't have much left to dispose of. If you have left over candle stubs I would recommend burying them or throwing them in the trash.

Personally, I prefer not to reuse candles that have already been used for a spell, they carry the intent from the previous working and it can cause a confused spell if you use it for another. Any herbs or natural items left over can be buried or thrown in the compost bin. If you have created an incense or oil blend with a specific intent and you have some left over, label it and keep it to use for another spell with the same intent.

A charming ending ...

All the information in this book is just to give you a starting point, take each spell and personalise it and make it your own. You don't need to spend lots of money to work spells, use whatever you have to hand and what works for you.

Trust your intuition.

The magic is within YOU.

Bibliography

Pagan Portals: Kitchen Witchcraft

Grimoire of a Kitchen Witch

Pagan Portals: Hoodoo Folk Magic

Pagan Portals: Moon Magic

A Kitchen Witch's World of Magical Plants & Herbs

A Kitchen Witch's World of Magical Foods

Pagan Portals: Meditation

The Art of Ritual

Arc of the Goddess (co-written with Tracey Roberts)

Pagan Portals: The Cailleach

Moon Books Gods & Goddesses Colouring Book (Patterson family)

Pagan Portals: Animal Magic

Witchcraft ... into the Wilds

Moon Books

PAGANISM & SHAMANISM

What is Paganism? A religion, a spirituality, an alternative belief system, nature worship? You can find support for all these definitions (and many more) in dictionaries, encyclopaedias, and text books of religion, but subscribe to any one and the truth will evade you. Above all Paganism is a creative pursuit, an encounter with reality, an exploration of meaning and an expression of the soul. Druids, Heathens, Wiccans and others, all contribute their insights and literary riches to the Pagan tradition. Moon Books invites you to begin or to deepen your own encounter, right here, right now.

If you have enjoyed this book, why not tell other readers by posting a review on your preferred book site. Recent bestsellers from Moon Books are:

Journey to the Dark Goddess
How to Return to Your Soul
Jane Meredith

Discover the powerful secrets of the Dark Goddess and transform your depression, grief and pain into healing and integration.

Paperback: 978-1-84694-677-6 ebook: 978-1-78099-223-5

Shamanic Reiki
Expanded Ways of Working with Universal Life Force Energy
Llyn Roberts, Robert Levy
Shamanism and Reiki are each powerful ways of healing; together,
their power multiplies. Shamanic Reiki introduces techniques to
help healers and Reiki practitioners tap ancient healing wisdom.
Paperback: 978-1-84694-037-8 ebook: 978-1-84694-650-9

Pagan Portals – The Awen Alone
Walking the Path of the Solitary Druid
Joanna van der Hoeven
An introductory guide for the solitary Druid, The Awen Alone
will accompany you as you explore, and seek out your own place
within the natural world.
Paperback: 978-1-78279-547-6 ebook: 978-1-78279-546-9

A Kitchen Witch's World of Magical Herbs & Plants
Rachel Patterson
A journey into the magical world of herbs and plants, filled with
magical uses, folklore, history and practical magic. By popular
writer, blogger and kitchen witch, Tansy Firedragon.
Paperback: 978-1-78279-621-3 ebook: 978-1-78279-620-6

Medicine for the Soul
The Complete Book of Shamanic Healing
Ross Heaven
All you will ever need to know about shamanic healing and how to
become your own shaman...
Paperback: 978-1-78099-419-2 ebook: 978-1-78099-420-8

Shaman Pathways – The Druid Shaman
Exploring the Celtic Otherworld
Danu Forest
A practical guide to Celtic shamanism with exercises and
techniques as well as traditional lore for exploring the Celtic
Otherworld.
Paperback: 978-1-78099-615-8 ebook: 978-1-78099-616-5

Traditional Witchcraft for the Woods and Forests
A Witch's Guide to the Woodland with Guided Meditations and
Pathworking
Melusine Draco
A Witch's guide to walking alone in the woods, with guided
meditations and pathworking.
Paperback: 978-1-84694-803-9 ebook: 978-1-84694-804-6

Wild Earth, Wild Soul
A Manual for an Ecstatic Culture
Bill Pfeiffer
Imagine a nature-based culture so alive and so connected,
spreading like wildfire. This book is the first flame...
Paperback: 978-1-78099-187-0 ebook: 978-1-78099-188-7

Naming the Goddess
Trevor Greenfield
Naming the Goddess is written by over eighty adherents and
scholars of Goddess and Goddess Spirituality.
Paperback: 978-1-78279-476-9 ebook: 978-1-78279-475-2

Shapeshifting into Higher Consciousness
Heal and Transform Yourself and Our World with Ancient
Shamanic and Modern Methods
Llyn Roberts
Ancient and modern methods that you can use every day to
transform yourself and make a positive difference in the world.
Paperback: 978-1-84694-843-5 ebook: 978-1-84694-844-2

Readers of ebooks can buy or view any of these bestsellers by
clicking on the live link in the title. Most titles are published in
paperback and as an ebook. Paperbacks are available in traditional
bookshops. Both print and ebook formats are available online.

Find more titles and sign up to our readers' newsletter at
http://www.johnhuntpublishing.com/paganism
Follow us on Facebook at https://www.facebook.com/MoonBooks
and Twitter at https://twitter.com/MoonBooksJHP